Predestined for HELL?

NO!

John R. Rice

Author of Prayer—Asking and Receiving; The Home—Courtship, Marriage, and Children; Power of Pentecost; Twelve Tremendous Themes; The Ruin of a Christian; King of the Jews; Coming Kingdom of Christ, etc.

D1713797

SWORD of the LORD
PUBLISHERS
P. O. BOX 1099, MURFREESBORO, TN 37133

Copyright 1958 by
Sword of the Lord Foundation
Renewal 1986

ISBN 0-87398-657-1

PRINTED IN U.S.A.

TABLE OF CONTENTS

Introduction

"For whom he did foreknow, he also did predestinate to be conformed to the image of his Son, that he might be the firstborn among many brethren."—Rom. 8:29.

Does God really predestinate some people to be saved and predestinate others to go to Hell, so that they have no free choice? Absolutely not! Nobody is predestined to be saved, except as he chooses, of his own free will, to repent of sin and trust Christ for salvation.

No one is predestined ahead of time to go to Hell. Christ died for the sins of the whole world. God is not willing that any should perish. Salvation is freely offered to "whosoever will."

After showing what Calvinism is and that it is a man-made philosophy, we plan to show by the Bible the following blessed facts:

Hyper-Calvinism Is a Man-Made Philosophy Not in the Scriptures;

God Makes Plans Ahead in History for Man and Nations;

Christ's Atoning Death Paid for the Sins of Every Person Ever Born;

God's Love, Enlightenment, Enabling and Invitation Reach Every Sinner;

Not a Single Soul Is Predestined Without an Opportunity to Be Saved;

God's Grace Not Irresistible;

Bible Doctrines Show Hyper-Calvinism Morally Impossible;

God Predestinates Those Who Will Trust in Christ to Land Safe at Last in Heaven!

The Harm Done by Hyper-Calvinism Heresy;

5

John Calvin, a great theologian, was right in saying that people are saved by grace alone and kept by grace alone. But extreme Calvinism, the teaching that some people, by the foreordained plan of God, are predestined to be saved and some are predestined to be lost, and that their destinies were settled before they were born, is a wicked heresy contrary to the Bible, that dishonors God and has done incalculable harm. The heresy of extreme Calvinism is particularly appealing to people from four viewpoints.

First, it appeals to the scholarly intellect, the self-sufficient and proud mind. So brilliant, philosophical, scholarly preachers are apt to be misled on this matter more than the humble-hearted Bible-believer.

Second, this doctrine appeals particularly to those who hold "covenant theology," that is, the Presbyterian doctrine that believers and their children should be received in the church alike, that babies sprinkled in infancy are in a covenant relationship with God without any choice of their own, etc.

Third, the hyper-Calvinistic heresy is particularly appealing to the carnal nature, unwilling to have the heartbreak, the burden for soul winning, unwilling to pay the price of separation and perhaps ostracism which goes with all-out soul winning, unwilling to pay the price for the fullness of the Spirit in continual self-crucifixion and waiting on God.

Fourth, Calvinism especially appeals to those who think that hyper-Calvinism is the only answer to Arminianism. They do not believe that a saved person is "on probation" and may lose his salvation at any moment. They know that the Bible clearly teaches salvation by grace and not of works. Hyper-Calvinists would like to make people believe, and to make many believe that, if one does not teach universal salvation, he must be either a Calvinist or an Arminian. The Arminian position does such violence to the grace of God, many would rather be Calvinists. I am convinced that Whitefield and Spurgeon were both influenced, by the pressure of Arminian theology in their day, to call themselves Calvinists, although neither was hyper-Calvinistic in actual practice and emphasis.

Note some of the foolish statements of hyper-Calvinists. It has been said that "there are babes in Hell not a span long," that is, little ones who died in infancy or before birth, predestined to Hell with no choice in the matter! That is wholly unscriptural.

A godly pastor in New Jersey told friends how he had been a wicked sinner until God in mercy convicted him and saved him; how near he had come to eternal ruin! But an arrogant and prominent hyper-Calvinist said to him, "Why, that time when you consciously turned to Christ was not when you were regenerated! You were saved when you were a babe in your mother's arms, or possibly before your birth. If you are a Christian, you were predestined to be saved."

I heard the same man tell missionaries in Japan, "Don't worry about people going to Hell because you didn't get the Gospel to them, or if you had no soul-winning power. Their salvation is in God's hands, not in yours." Also he said, "If you are saved now, there never was any danger of your going to Hell." You can imagine whether such teaching is helpful in making soul winners!

But if we take the Scriptures at face value and believe them in childlike faith, how blessed is the teaching of the Bible on God's foreknowledge, foreordination, predestination, and election.

Chapter I

John Calvin's Theory
of Predestination

There is a Bible doctrine of God's foreknowledge, predestination and election. Most great bodies of Christians, not strictly Calvinists, or not Calvinists at all, agree that God has His controlling hand on the affairs of men. They agree that, according to the Bible, He selects individuals like Abraham, Isaac, Jacob, David, and King Cyrus, as instruments to do certain things He has planned. He raised up Pharaoh who was already "a vessel of wrath," with many years of hardened heart and wicked rejection, to make him an example of punishment. Christians agree that God may choose a nation, particularly that He did choose Israel, through which He would give the law, the prophets, and eventually through whom the Saviour would come. It is a Bible doctrine that God foreknows who will trust in Christ, and that He has predestined or purposed to see that they are justified and glorified. He will keep the saved, will glorify those He saves. You see, Calvin did not originate those teachings. They are taught in the Bible, believed by multitudes who are not Calvinists.

But the doctrine that God predestined some men to Hell, that some cannot be saved, that they are born to be damned by God's own choice, is a doctrine of Calvinism, a philosophy developed by John Calvin. It is a sectarian tenet strictly followed only by hyper-Calvinists. It is a radical heresy, not taught in the Bible.

The term *Calvinism* is loosely used by people who do not hold Calvin's teaching on predestination. To thousands who may call themselves Calvinists, the word means only that they believe in salvation by grace, without human merit, as Calvin did, and so believe in everlasting life for the believer, since he is kept by the power of God. One who says he is a Calvinist generally means simply that he is not an Arminian, that he is kept by the grace of God, and is not saved or kept by his own works or life.

So those who are generally, but mistakenly, called Calvinists only rarely follow Calvin in his doctrine that some are predestined to be lost, born to be damned, by God's own plan, and cannot be saved.

I. Calvin Taught That Some Are Ordained, Predestined to Hell, Cannot Be Saved

I have before me the large authoritative book, *The Reformed Doctrine of Predestination,* by Dr. Loraine Boettner. In a chapter entitled, "The Five Points of Calvinism," he says the following: "The Calvinistic system especially emphasizes five distinct doctrines. These are technically known as 'The Five Points of Calvinism,' and they are the main pillars upon which the superstructure rests."

Now what are these five points? Dr. Boettner says: "The Five Points may be more easily remembered if they are associated with the word T-U-L-I-P; T, Total Inability; U, Unconditional Election; L, Limited Atonement; I, Irresistible (Efficacious) Grace; and P, Perseverance of the Saints."

Note the language. Four of the points named are expressly worded to teach that some are ordained to be damned. There is in the book mentioned a separate chapter on each of the five points following, explaining their meaning to be so.

By "Total Inability," Calvin meant and Dr. Boettner means that a lost sinner cannot repent, cannot believe unless he is foreordained to repent and unless God overpowers him, and that God has chosen not to overpower many.

By "Unconditional Election," Calvin meant and Dr. Boettner and all hyper-Calvinists mean that people are elected to be saved without any reference to anything they may do, and people are foreordained to be damned, unconditionally. By "Limited Atonement," the strict Calvinists mean, as John Calvin did, that Christ really died only for those who are ordained to be saved, and that He did not atone for the sins of those He has ordained to be lost.

By "Irresistible Grace," Calvin meant that it is foolish to urge people to decide, because those who are ordained to be saved will be irresistibly moved and overpowered by God's grace, and so will be saved.

Some reader unacquainted with this subject and unfamiliar with Calvin's doctrines may believe that we have overstated the doctrine. It so obviously disagrees with the oft-repeated invitations in the Bible to all sinners to come to Christ and be saved that some will think we have misrepresented Calvinism. But a casual study of the documents available will show that we are very carefully giving the meaning of extreme Calvinism, that is, the Calvinistic doctrine that some are predestined to be damned, that God did not intend for them to be saved, and that they cannot be saved.

John Calvin in his *Institutes*, Book III, Chapter 23, says, ". . . Not all men are created with a similar destiny but eternal life is foreordained for some, and eternal damnation for others. Every man, therefore, being created for one or the other of these ends, we say, he is predestined either to life or to death." And further Calvin says, "There can be no election without its opposition, reprobation."

Loraine Boettner in *The Reformed Doctrine of Predestination*, says, "The doctrine of absolute Predestination of course logically holds that some are foreordained to death as truly as others are foreordained to life." And then he says, "This, too, is of God. We believe that from all eternity God has intended to leave some of Adam's posterity in their sins, and that the decisive factor in the life of each is to be found only in God's will."

The Westminster Confession, which is the best-known and most widely held Presbyterian creed, states this: "By the decree of God, for the manifestation of His glory, some men and angels are predestinated to everlasting life and others are foreordained to everlasting death."

So hyper-Calvinism teaches that it is God's own choice

that some people are to be damned forever. He never intended to save them. He foreordained them to be damned.
When He offers mercy in the Bible, He does it with the
plain knowledge that some men cannot accept it, because He
will not help them to accept it. So says the extreme Calvinist.

This doctrine insists that we need not urge a man to
turn to Christ. He cannot turn until God forces him to do so.
If God has planned for him to be eternally lost, he will not
be turned to God. If God has planned for him to be saved,
then "irresistible grace," the hyper-Calvinist says, will
force him to be saved.

This is stated in the book, *"Whosoever Will,"* by Professor Herman Hoeksema, in these words:

> "That work is absolutely divine. Man has no part in
> it, and cannot possibly co-operate with God in his own
> salvation. In no sense of the word, and at no stage of
> the work, does salvation depend upon the will or work
> of man, or wait for the determination of his will. In
> fact, the sinner is of himself neither capable nor will-
> ing to receive that salvation. On the contrary, all he
> can do and will is to oppose, to resist his own salvation
> with all the determination of his sinful heart. But God
> ordained, and prepared this salvation with absolutely
> sovereign freedom for His own, His chosen ones alone,
> and upon them He bestows it, not because they seek
> and desire it, but in spite of the fact that they never
> will it, and because He is stronger than man, and over-
> comes the hardest heart and the most stubborn will
> of the sinner."

That is not evangelical Christianity; that is not the
Bible doctrine that God is "not willing that any should
perish, but that all should come to repentance" (II Pet. 3:9).
It is not the doctrine that "whosoever will, let him take the
water of life freely" (Rev. 22:17), but it is the philosophy
or teaching of hyper-Calvinists.

However, it is fair to say that Calvin is thought to
have modified his views somewhat through the years. Dr.

Augustus H. Strong, in his standard Systematic Theology, Vol. III Doctrine of Salvation, page 778, quotes Calvin's later comments to prove this, as follows:

"The progress in Calvin's thought may be seen by comparing some of his earlier with his later utterances. Institutes, 2:23:5—'I say, with Augustine, that the Lord created those who, as he certainly foreknew, were to go to destruction, and he did so because he so willed.' But even then in the Institutes, 3:23:8, he affirms that 'the perdition of the wicked depends upon the divine predestination in such a manner that the cause and matter of it are found in themselves. Man falls by the appointment of divine providence, but he falls by his own fault.' God's blinding, hardening, turning the sinner he describes as the consequence of the divine DESERTION, not the divine CAUSATION. The relation of God to the origin of sin is not efficient, but permissive. In later days Calvin wrote in his Commentary on I John 2:2—'he is the propitiation for our sins; and not for ours only, but also for the whole world'—as follows:

" 'Christ suffered for the sins of the whole world, and in the goodness of God is offered unto all men without distinction, his blood being shed not for a part of the world only, but for the whole human race; for although in the world nothing is found worthy of the favor of God, yet he holds out the propitiation to the whole world, since without exception he summons all to the faith of Christ, which is nothing else than the door unto hope.'

"Although other passages, such as Institutes, 3:21:5, and 3:23:1, assert the harsher view, we must give Calvin credit for modifying his doctrine with maturer reflection and advancing years. Much that is called Calvinism would have been repudiated by Calvin himself even at the beginning of his career, and is really the exaggeration of his teaching by more scholastic and less religious successors. Renan calls Calvin 'the most Christian man of his generation.' Dorner describes him as 'equally great in intellect and character, lovely in social life, full of tender sympathy and faithfulness to his friends, yielding and forgiving toward personal offences.' The device upon his seal is a flaming heart from which is stretched forth a helping hand."

So when we speak of hyper-Calvinism we mean Calvinism gone to extremes, not necessarily Calvin's more mature thought but the earlier radical position, and particularly the extreme position and hurtful heresy held by many followers of Calvin.

II. This Teaching That God Ordains Some to Hell, Some Who Cannot Be Saved, Is a Strictly Sectarian Teaching

Is hyper-Calvinism a general Bible doctrine, recognized by honest Bible believers of many faiths? Is it taught in undenominational, evangelical colleges, seminaries, Bible institutes? Is it an accepted teaching among sound Bible teachers and recognized Bible conferences? It is not. Hyper-Calvinism is a distinctly sectarian teaching, held by a few who follow a particular man-made creed. It is not held by Bible-believing Christians in various denominations, but only by followers of John Calvin. I do not say that these hyper-Calvinists are dishonest; I do not say that they do not intend to follow the Scriptures. But I say that they are biased by sectarian spirit. They are influenced by a human creed, and have a sectarian and biased viewpoint.

For example, I have before me the book by Dr. Loraine Boettner, *The Reformed Doctrine of Predestination*. This book is greatly valued by hyper-Calvinists. It has gone through eight editions since 1932, has 432 large pages, is a recognized textbook on the subject.

But note that this doctrine is called "the reformed doctrine" of predestination. In other words, predestination, as here taught, is a doctrine of the reformed faith, that is, a doctrine as held by Presbyterian and Reformed churches.

It would be only natural for some Catholic to write a book on "the Catholic doctrine of the mass." That would cause no surprise because the doctrine of the mass is a sectarian doctrine of the Roman church. A book on "the Mormon doctrine of plural marriages" would be suitable because the doctrine that God ordained for Mormon men to

marry as many wives as they could so they would have more
wives in Heaven is a Mormon doctrine. It is not a generally
accepted, evangelical doctrine that cuts across all evangelical
denominations. It is not a Bible doctrine. And so the term,
"The Reformed Doctrine of Predestination," accepted and
widely used by those who believe in that doctrine, indicates
that it is really a sectarian doctrine.

But a second name, even more widely used for this particular doctrine that some are predestined to be damned by
the plan of God, is *Calvinism*. That means that this doctrine
was formulated by Calvin, and those who hold it get it from
Calvin. And their statement of faith follows exactly and literally every doctrinal position of Calvin.

I am saying that this hyper-Calvinistic position is a
sectarian doctrine.

A sectarian viewpoint is fatal to an unbiased approach
to the Scriptures. Any doctrine to be accepted by Bible believers ought to be one which is plainly found in the Bible
itself by honest seekers with open hearts, whether from any
denomination or no denomination. In my book, *Bible Baptism*, I expressly state that I am not interested in teaching
what Baptists believe about baptism or why pedobaptists
are wrong on baptism; I am interested only in teaching
what the Bible teaches about baptism. A strict denominational pride would color everything found in the Bible and
make one's teaching unreliable.

All over America, Bible institutes which are interdenominational in character, fundamental and orthodox, find
certain great doctrines clearly taught in the Bible. It may be
surprising to some, but the doctrine of salvation by grace,
without works, and the kindred doctrine of God's faithful
keeping of born-again Christians and their eternal security
are clearly taught in Bible institutes and undenominational
seminaries over the world. You see, these doctrines are
found in the Bible. A man who is an ardent Presbyterian, or
a Baptist, or a Pentecostalist, or one of Christian and Missionary Alliance background, for example, may find this doctrine in the Bible. Some honest people differ, but certainly
the matter of salvation by grace through faith, and God's

merciful keeping of His saints by grace, is not a sectarian doctrine. Now Calvin believed in these doctrines of grace. They are found in the Bible. But Calvin's doctrine about "reprobation," that is, that God has foreordained and planned that some people should be damned, is not an evangelical doctrine found in the Bible by honest Bible believers of all faiths or of most faiths. It is a sectarian doctrine held only by those who follow Calvin's philosophy.

That hyper-Calvinism is a sectarian doctrine is illustrated by the other doctrines that go with it. For example, I was in a service to approve a statement of faith for the National Association of Evangelicals. It was agreed the statement of faith should require a belief in "the new birth." But when I suggested that in the statement of faith we should say "saved by grace through faith," the committee was warned that we should leave out "by faith," because Dutch Reformed people who are strict Calvinists insist that those who are foreordained to be saved are saved irresistibly, without any exercise of the will, without any co-operation with God, and that some are saved in babyhood or in their mothers' wombs! I say this illustrates that hyper-Calvinism is a sectarian doctrine, held by members of a sect and goes with other sectarian doctrines.

To show the bias, the limited and prejudiced sectarian viewpoint of hyper-Calvinists, let me give an example of typical hyper-Calvinistic argument.

Dr. Loraine Boettner, in *The Reformed Doctrine of Predestination*, page 47, says, "There are really only three systems which claim to set forth a way of salvation through Christ." And he names them: 1. Universalism, that all will be saved; 2. Arminianism, "which holds that Christ died equally and indiscriminately for every individual . . . , that saving grace is not necessarily permanent, but that those who are loved of God, ransomed by Christ, and born again of the Holy Spirit, may (let God wish and strive ever so much to the contrary) throw away all and perish eternally"; and 3. Calvinism. Note that Dr. Boettner, with other hyper-Calvinists, states that "there are really only three systems which claim to set forth a way of salvation through Christ."

He says, "Only two are held by Christians, that is, Calvin's position and Arminius' position.

Does not this show that Dr. Boettner, with other radical hyper-Calvinists, is either totally unaware of the vast mass of evangelical literature on this subject and the position of most orthodox Christians in the world, or that he is so biased that he plays down the facts and omits them in this case? That is the viewpoint of a narrow-minded, warped sectarian.

Do you really believe that the only two systems of doctrine concerning the way of salvation aside from universalism, which, he admits, "has never been held by an organized Christian church," are Arminianism and hyper-Calvinism? (He means Calvinism as taught by Calvin himself and by the Westminster Catechism involving Cadvin's doctrine of predestination.)

The simple truth is that probably not one out of ten, even of Presbyterians, in the United States believe in Calvin's position on the matter of salvation. Almost no Baptists believe that. And yet these groups are not Arminian. The Bible institutes, the independent Christian colleges in America are generally not Arminian, yet they do not hold to Calvin's position of strict predestination, limited atonement, irresistible grace, and that God planned some to be eternally damned. Most of the best Christians in America, the most devout Bible believers, are neither strict Calvinists nor Arminians.

The great evangelists and soul winners have usually been men who were not Arminian, because they believed in salvation by grace, without works. Moody, Torrey, Chapman, Truett, Billy Sunday, Bob Jones, Jack Hyles, for example; none of them have been Arminian. They have not believed that a born-again child of God, saved by grace, will fall away and be lost. They did not claim to be Arminian, and Arminians do not claim them.

Yet none of these men believed that people are saved by irresistible grace without any reference to their own choice, or that God has foreordained others to be damned without a chance to be saved.

The statement of Calvinists on this matter is simply unreliable. Dr. Boettner is foolishly, utterly mistaken. The doctrine of strict Calvinism involves a biased, partial, sectarian viewpoint. And the doctrine is stated with the bias and passion of sectarians. It is not Bible doctrine but sectarian doctrine.

III. Few Evangelical Christians Hold This Extreme Predestination Doctrine

When large claims are made about how many groups of Christians are Calvinists, the reader must bear in mind that in general terms, as most Christians use this word, Calvinism does not refer to this radical predestination doctrine of Calvin, but to the doctrines of salvation by grace, the security of a born-again child of God, kept by God's power. As we have said before, great masses of Christians believe that man is a fallen creature who cannot save himself, that man is depraved, dead in trespasses and sins, and that only the grace of God can save such a sinner, even as Calvin believed. The great masses of orthodox, Bible-believing Christians agree that God has plans in this world and has His hands on the affairs of men. They know that God has chosen the nation Israel, has chosen certain individuals for certain tasks. They believe that God has known ahead of time who will come to love and trust Him, that He has predestined these to be conformed to the image of His Son, as we are plainly told in Romans 8:29. But they are not Calvinists as regards predestination.

Dr. Boettner in his textbook, *The Reformed Doctrine of Predestination*, lists as Calvinistic the Baptist and Congregational Churches, the Established Church of England, the Episcopal Church in America, Lutherans, and Puritans, as well as Presbyterian and Reformed Churches. He even says, "This faith was for a time held by the Roman Catholic Church, and at no time has that church ever openly repudiated it."

But that does not mean that all these church bodies or all the Christians involved, or that even any considerable

fraction of the Christians involved, believe in the radical
hyper-Calvinistic doctrine of predestination. They certainly
do not. In fact, Boettner plainly admits this. He says, "It
is only rarely that we now come across those who can be
called 'Calvinists without reserve.' " The more independent
Bible study increases and the more scriptural evangelism
we have, the less do people believe in this hyper-Calvinistic
doctrine of predestination.

Do Baptists believe in "The Five Points of Calvinism"?
They do not. Many years ago there was a division among
Baptists in the southern United States on this subject. The
two bodies were called "Primitive Baptists" and "Missionary
Baptists." There are now 8 million Southern Baptists, many
other Missionary Baptists, but only a handful of Primitive
Baptists, not more than a very few thousand. It is a dying
group. And all the other millions of Baptists in Baptist
bodies, with rare individual exceptions, repudiate hyper-
Calvinism. Conservative Baptists, the General Association
of Regular Baptists, the American Baptist Convention,
Swedish Baptists, German Baptists—all these, perhaps 16
million Baptists in America—are not Arminian, but they
are not actual Calvinists. Only the Free Will Baptist group in
the States and the small group of Reformed Baptists in
Canada hold to the Arminian position. None but the small
"Primitive Baptist" group, called sometimes "Hard-Shell
Baptists," are strict Calvinists. The other millions hold to
salvation by grace, and the other great doctrines of grace
of evangelical Christianity, but they disagree heartily with
Calvin's Five Points, in his radical teaching on predestination.

In the interdenominational, fundamental movement in America represented by Moody Bible Institute, Bible Institute of Los
Angeles, Tennessee Temple, Bob Jones University, Baptist Bible
College, the great Bible institutes of the Christian and Missionary Alliance, etc., and in the many, many other interdenominational, fundamental Bible institutes and Bible colleges, you will find almost no teachers who are hyper-Calvinists
and, I think, not a single statement of faith taking the hyper-

Calvinist position. So the claims of the predestinarians on this matter are wrong.

Wherever people gather without the bias of a sectarian denominational spirit, and study the Bible with earnest, believing hearts, then hyper-Calvinism loses out as it has lost out in the fundamental Bible institutes of America, on the principal Bible conference programs of America, in the principal interdenominational Christian magazines in America, and in the great revivals of leading soul winners. On the fringes of the fundamentalist movement, only one well-known man, an active defender of his modernistic denomination and a worker with the National Council of Churches, a defender of procommunist church leaders of Czechoslovakia and other countries, is an ardent hyper-Calvinist. But he has that position because he is literally a sectarian Calvinist, a Reformed Presbyterian, following the Westminster Catechism. He did not get his position as an independent, fundamental Christian. So there are few evangelical Christians holding the hyper-Calvinistic viewpoint.

Chapter II

Hyper-Calvinism Is a Man-Made Philosophy Not in the Scriptures

To be sure, Calvin and those who followed Calvin claimed to believe and follow the Bible. They claimed to find at least a germ of the hyper-Calvinist doctrine of predestination, that some are elected to be saved irresistibly, and others are foreordained to be damned, in the Scriptures. But a careful student will find that again and again they go beyond Scripture and that hyper-Calvinism is a philosophy developed by men and depending on fallible logic and frail human reason, with the perversion of some Scriptures, the misuse of other Scriptures, and the total ignoring of still other Scriptures.

Calvin did teach many wonderful true doctrines of Scripture. It is true that God foreknows everything that will happen in the world. It is true that He definitely ordained and determined *some* events ahead of time, and selected *some* individuals for His purposes. It is certain that people are saved only by the grace of God, and kept by the grace of God. That far Calvinists may well prove their doctrines by the Scriptures. But beyond that, hyper-Calvinism goes into a realm of human philosophy. It is not a Bible doctrine, but a system of human philosophy appealing somewhat to the proud mind. Those who know that they are saved and saved forever feel very superior to others who, they think, are elected to be damned. But that is a human philosophy, not a Bible teaching.

And that, I think, we can show to honest and open hearts.

I. Hyper-Calvinism Was Developed By Calvin

Consider first that what we are discussing is called "Calvinism." Dr. Loraine Boettner says, "It was Calvin who wrought out this system of theological thought with such logical clearness and emphasis that it has ever since borne his name" (*The Reformed Doctrine of Predestination*). Warburton says, "But inasmuch as it was Calvin who first formulated these principles into a more or less complete system, that system, or creed, if you will, and likewise those principles which are embodied in it, came to bear his name" (*Calvinism*).

How strange that, after 1,400 years of Christianity, practically no one had understood the Bible to teach Calvin's doctrine of predestination until he formed the philosophy!

Again, notice these statements by Dr. Boettner:

"It may occasion some surprise to discover that the doctrine of Predestination was not made a matter of special study until near the end of the fourth century. The earlier church fathers placed chief emphasis on good works such as faith, repentance, almsgiving, prayers, submission to baptism, etc., as the basis of salvation. They of course taught that salvation was through Christ; yet they assumed that man had full power to accept or reject the gospel" (page 365, *The Reformed Doctrine of Predestination*).

Again he says, "This cardinal truth of Christianity [he means predestination] was first clearly seen by Augustine, the great Spirit-filled theologian of the West."

Again Boettner says, "Following Augustine there was retrogression rather than progress."

(That is, there was retrogression in the teaching of predestination.) Then, we are taught, a thousand years went by before the doctrine of predestination was again resurrected and carefully formulated by Calvin!

What a strangely hidden doctrine, that New Testament Christians could go for nearly four hundred years and nobody find it in the Bible or teach it until Augustine is supposed to have seen it. And then the doctrine was hidden again for a thousand years until the days of the reformers, when Calvin developed the doctrine fully.

It is obvious that great groups of Christians have always found salvation by grace in the Bible. The Bible is very clear on that. It is clear on every other great doctrine. Then if there is only one man in four hundred years, and another man after a thousand years to find the Calvinistic doctrine of predestination in the Bible, it surely must not be a clearly taught Bible doctrine! No, Calvinism is a philosophy of men which is not primarily based upon the Bible. It is based upon the logic and philosophy of a man, with some misinterpretations of Scriptures and ignoring great numbers of plain statements of Scriptures.

Take, for example, the "Five Points of Calvinism." Who can find these five points listed in the Bible? Where does the Bible indicate that there are any definite and exclusive five points as a foundation for theology? That organization of thought comes from Calvin, not from the Bible. It is a human philosophy, not a Bible doctrine.

II. Calvinism the Product of an Age Now Gone

Note the Calvinistic appraisal of possible doctrines on salvation. Calvinism claims (*The Reformed Doctrine of Predestination*, Boettner, page 47) that "There are really only three systems which claim to set forth a way of salvation through Christ." And he says that they are Universalism, Arminianism, and Calvinism, by which he means the Calvinistic position of the "Five Points," including radical hyper-Calvinistic predestination.

That organization of thought, that outline, arose hundreds of years ago when Calvinism was at its height, influencing Lutherans, Puritans, and others. Arminianism was very strong. John Wesley had his magazine, *The Arminian.* The great modern missionary movement had not been born, the great evangelists, Moody, Torrey, Chapman, Billy Sunday, had not appeared on the scene. The interdenominational Bible institutes and Christian colleges had not come into being. The Bible conference movement, with independent, undenominational Bible study, free and widespread without the bondage of sectarianism, had not come. According to the appearances and logic of men hundreds of years ago, aside from Universalism, there appeared to be only two basic positions concerning salvation; that is, Arminianism, free will—one could be saved when he chose and be lost again tomorrow, etc.—or Calvinism, which, in that time, meant predestination and all.

But now every sensible person knows that human philosophy which grew out of an age and the dominating, overpowering influence of John Calvin himself, is simply a human system. It does not represent the teachings of the Bible and does not represent Christianity. It is an obsolete human philosophy which never did properly represent the Scriptures. Now most of the Bible teachers, the ministers, the soul winners, and the theologians in the world would be outside those three classifications. You see, it never was a scriptural classification, for extreme Calvinism is a man-made philosophy, not a Bible doctrine.

III. Calvinism Is a Philosophy Of Human Reason, Not Divine Revelation

The writings of the hyper-Calvinists abound in terms like "then it must logically follow that . . . ." The doctrine is based on a system of human reasoning. For example, the hyper-Calvinist reasons that if God foreknew what would occur, then He must have ordered it. If He knew sin would come, then He must have planned the sin. Of course the Bible never says that. It is a conclusion based only on the human reason.

Boettner argues that if any person has a choice and may decide right or wrong on moral issues, then God Himself would not know how things would turn out. "He would then be ignorant of much of the future and would daily be gaining vast stores of knowledge. His government of the world also, in that case, would be very uncertain and changeable, dependent as it would be, on the unforeseen conduct of men." Note that here the doctrine is wholly based on a human argument; if God did not arbitrarily decide what men must do, and leave them no choice of their own, then, says Boettner, God Himself would be ignorant of what was going to occur! That is a sample of the human arguments and logic on which this unscriptural doctrine is based. It is a philosophy of men, not a Bible teaching.

IV. The Terminology of Calvinism Is Not Bible Terminology

That it is human philosophy instead of a Bible doctrine is indicated also by the very language which is used.

The strict unreserved Calvinist teaches a doctrine which he calls "reprobation," that is, that some men are condemned to Hell, foreordained to damnation before they are born, and that they cannot believe, cannot repent, cannot be saved, by God's own deliberate choice. I say that in the writings of predestinarians like Boettner, in the International Standard Bible Encyclopedia in the article written by a Calvinist on predestination, and throughout Calvinist literature, this name "Reprobation" is given to the doctrine. But such a name is not even found in Scripture nor implied in Scripture. The Bible has no doctrine of "reprobation," and the Bible does not use that word, nor any word like it, in reference to predestination. It is a human word for a human conception. Neither the language nor the doctrine it represents is inspired or taken from the Word of God.

Take the names of the "Five Points" of Calvinism: Total Inability, Unconditional Election, Limited Atonement, Irresistible Grace, Perseverance of the Saints. A study of these words will show how far they differ from the language of Scripture.

There is a doctrine of the depravity of the fallen race of men and that there is nothing good in man to earn or deserve salvation or make him capable of earning it. That is true, as all students of Scripture assent. But the Bible does not call this "total inability." In fact, the Bible never even hints that there are many people who have no ability to be saved. The Bible teaches that a man may so harden his heart and go on in his sins that his mind may be darkened and God may turn him over to a reprobate mind as a result of his own rejection of the Gospel. But the idea that many men, women and children are totally unable to repent, and always have been; that they are unable to choose for Christ, unable to believe in Him, is not a scriptural doctrine. The language itself is not scriptural.

"Unconditional election" means, to a Calvinist, that God has already decided who will be saved and it has no reference as to whether he wishes to be saved or not. God has already decided who will go to Hell and it has no reference to anything he will decide for himself. The election to Heaven or Hell is unconditional, wholly on God's part, says the Calvinist. But is there any such language in the Bible? There is not! It is true that God, in mercy, elects some men to do certain tasks, since He knows that they will obey Him in these matters. In that matter, "it is not of him that runneth but of God that showeth mercy." But concerning all men everywhere, and *on the matter of salvation,* the Bible has no teaching of "unconditional election," and the language itself is not Bible language.

Calvinists insist on point three, "Limited Atonement." They mean that Christ died only for the elect. For those that He planned and ordained should go to Hell, He did not die, they say. But such language is never used in the Bible. And the doctrine wholly contradicts many plain Scriptures like, "He is the propitiation for our sins: and not for our's only, but also for the sins of the whole world" (I John 2:2). It contradicts the express statement of Scripture, ". . . the man Christ Jesus; Who gave himself a ransom for all. . ." (I Tim. 2:5, 6). "Limited atonement" is not a Bible term because it does not represent a Bible doctrine. It represents a philosophy of men.

The fourth point of Calvinism is "Irresistible Grace." But the term "irresistible" is never used as a modifier of "grace" in the Bible. That terminology is not Bible terminology. The idea, the doctrine involved, is not a Bible idea, a Bible doctrine. The Bible represents the grace of God as loving mercy offered to all men. But Calvinism represents grace as the irresistible act of God compelling a man to be saved who does not want to be saved, so that a man has no choice in the matter except as God forcibly puts a choice in his mind. As Professor Herman Hoeksema says in *Whosoever Will,* "That work is absolutely divine. Man has no part in it, and cannot possibly cooperate with God in his own salvation. In no sense of the word, and at no stage of the work, does salvation depend upon the will or work of man, or wait for the determination of his will." No, irresistible grace, according to the philosophy of John Calvin, means that God simply forces some people to be saved, as He determines that others will be lost. But that is not the Bible doctrine of grace.

Even in the matter of God's blessed keeping of His saints, Calvinism uses terminology that is questionable. The fifth point of Calvinism is "Perseverance of the Saints." Now there is a great and blessed truth here, but the truth is that God preserves His saints, not so much that they persevere. My certainty of Heaven is not that God has compelled me by His overweening predestination to act a certain way; no, my security in Christ and the certainty of my eternal salvation depends not on my perseverance but on God's preservation. You see, Calvinism, this human philosophy, must put forth its tenets even to color any true doctrine it teaches. But the philosophy itself is unscriptural. The language of the doctrine is unscriptural because it represents an unscriptural position.

V. Arminianism, Like Calvinism, Uses Unscriptural Terminology

We ought to say here very plainly that Arminians likewise do wrong in using unscriptural language. It is true that God holds man to account to choose for right against the wrong, to repent and be saved, and to try to please God after he is saved. Man has "freedom of the will" in the sense that he can, by God's help, do what God has told him to do. But to insist that the freedom of the will is never affected on the one hand by sin or on the other hand by the grace of God, is wrong.

For example, a lost sinner may have free will, and can be saved, but if he goes on in sin, his heart may become so hardened and his mind so set in sin that eventually the man cannot be saved. God does not promise that a man will always be left so it is just as easy to do right as it is to do wrong. There comes a time when a man is so colored and hardened by his own wrong decisions that he is enslaved by sin; and sometimes God even turns a man over to his reprobate mind, to be damned. So Arminians make much of free will in a sense that makes it a human philosophy, not a Bible teaching.

Likewise Arminians argue that if one can trust Christ and be saved, he can later sin and be lost. But that ignores the clear Bible teaching that when one trusts in Jesus Christ for salvation he is changed. He becomes a partaker of the divine nature. The Holy Spirit of God moves into his body to live. He is now born of God. And that part of him which is saved, the new nature, cannot sin. The truth is that a part of a man's freedom is gone when he is saved, because a great change has taken place in his nature. No one has any freedom of the will that can undo the miraculous work of God's grace in making a child of wrath into a child of God.

Likewise, the Arminian language about "probation" is unscriptural. The idea that man is not ever really saved while on earth but is simply "on probation," and that at any time he may fail in his probation and then be damned, is an unscriptural doctrine. And the terminology itself is not Bible terminology. The Bible never anywhere says that a Christian is on probation. The language is human language because the doctrine is a human philosophy. You see, Arminianism, like hyper-Calvinism, is a human philosophy.

The simple truth is that God has provided salvation for all who will come to Christ, will repent of their sins and trust Him for salvation. But it is also true that He keeps those He saves. Salvation is of grace and not of works.

Why not just be a Bible Christian instead of being an Arminian or a Calvinist? Why should any man follow either Calvin or Arminius? Why should anybody let his doctrine be settled, on the one hand, by the Westminster Catechism, or, on the other hand, by the teachings of John Wesley?

VI. Calvinism Based on Misuse of Scripture

What Scripture does the hyper-Calvinist depend on principally for teaching that some are foreordained to be damned? Generally it is upon Romans 9:10-18.

Let us read that passage and then give a typical Calvinist comment upon it, to show this misuse of Scripture.

"And not only this; but when Rebecca also had conceived by one even by our father Isaac; (For the children being not yet born, neither having done any good or evil, that the purpose of God according to election might stand, not of works, but of him that calleth;) It was said unto her, The elder shall serve the younger. As it is written, Jacob have I loved, but Esau have I hated. What shall we say then? Is there unrighteousness with God? God forbid. For he saith to Moses, I will have mercy on whom I will have mercy, and I will have compassion on whom I will have compassion. So then it is not of him that willeth, nor of him

*that runneth, but of God that sheweth mercy. For the scrip-
ture saith unto Pharaoh, Even for this same purpose have
I raised thee up, that I might shew my power in thee, and
that my name might be declared throughout all the earth.
Therefore hath he mercy on whom he will have mercy, and
whom he will he hardeneth.*"

Now where does the hyper-Calvinist go wrong on this
Scripture?

Let us quote here the comment on verses 11 and 12 by
Warfield of Princeton in *Biblical Doctrines*. Warfield says:

"We are pointed illustratively to the sovereign ac-
ceptance of Isaac and rejection of Ishmael, and to the
choice of Jacob and not of Esau before their birth and
therefore before either had done good or bad; we are
explicitly told that *in the matter of salvation* it is not
of him that wills, or of him that runs, but of God that
shows mercy, and that He has mercy on whom
He will, and whom He will He hardens; we are
pointedly directed to behold in God the potter
who makes the vessels which proceed from His
hand each for an end of His appointment, that He may
work out His will upon them. It is safe to say that language cannot be chosen better adapted to teach Predestination at its height." (italics ours)

You will understand that Warfield is here particularly
teaching the predestination taught by Calvin and by the
Westminster Catechism, including the doctrine of "reprobation," the doctrine that some are predestined to be
damned.

Now where is Warfield's mistake? And Calvin's mistake?

It is in one phrase. In the midst of the quotation above,
Warfield says, "We are explicitly told that IN THE MAT-
TER OF SALVATION it is not of him that wills, or of him
that runs, but of God that shows mercy . . ." (capitals ours).

But we are explicitly told nothing of the kind! That entire passage of Scripture we have read above does not even
mention salvation. When God chose Isaac to be the head of

the nation Israel instead of Ishmael, it was not a "matter of salvation." When God chose Jacob instead of Esau to have the birthright and the headship of the nation, it had nothing to do with salvation.

When God raised up Pharaoh and made an issue with Pharaoh and so hardened Pharaoh's heart, it had nothing to do with salvation. God sent Moses to Pharaoh with a message. It was not, "Will you repent and be saved?" No, it was, "Let my people go." Pharaoh hardened his own heart, and God made an issue and caused him to be stubborn on the matter of whether or not he would release the slaves, stop his murder of innocent children, stop his exploitation of the poor, and let the Israelites go as God demanded. Already this wicked murderer had long hardened his heart against God as far as salvation is concerned.

Salvation is not the question under discussion in this passage at all. And Warfield and Calvin and all others who say that "we are explicitly told that in the matter of salvation" a person cannot will to be saved, but God decides arbitrarily to show mercy, he is teaching simply what the Bible does not teach. That is a perversion and misuse of Scripture. There are no Scriptures which teach hyper-Calvinism.

Hyper-Calvinism is not a Bible doctrine. It is a philosophy of men.

Chapter III

God Makes Plans Ahead in History for Man and Nations

It is clear from even a casual reading of the Bible that God does have His hand on the affairs of men. God does move things and people from behind the scenes. God does have plans ahead of time and works His will in many, many matters in the affairs of men.

That God knows all the future is clearly illustrated by

Bible prophecy. God had men to write down, often centuries ahead of time, things that would come to pass. For example, in Daniel, chapter 2, we have a brief but very clear outline of history. God said there would appear in succession four great world empires. This vision was given to King Nebuchadnezzar, the emperor of the first empire and through divine help interpreted by the Prophet Daniel. But Nebuchadnezzar's great Babylon was to be followed successively by other world empires—Media-Persia, Greece under Alexander the Great, and Rome.

A great image represented the Gentile world governments. The head was of gold but succeeding empires were of silver, brass, iron, and part iron and clay. Again, the Roman Empire is clearly pictured by the two legs, representing the division into the eastern and western portions of the Empire. Then the nations coming out of the Roman Empire and succeeding it are illustrated by the ten toes of the image. A similar prophecy is indicated by the four beasts in Daniel, chapter 7. God knows all history before it is written, all human affairs before they occur. Not only are these matters known to God; in large measure they are planned and ordained of God. When Nebuchadnezzar's heart was lifted up with pride and he said, "Is not this great Babylon, that I have built for the house of the kingdom by the might of my power, and for the honour of my majesty?" (Dan. 4:30), then God humbled Nebuchadnezzar. God took away his power, even his reason, caused him to eat grass in the field like an ox. He was demented seven years for this purpose, as God said, "until thou know that the most High ruleth in the kingdom of men, and giveth it to whomsoever he will" (Dan. 4:32). For His purpose, God moves kings and empires as well as individuals.

As Proverbs 21:1 says, "The king's heart is in the hand of the Lord, as the rivers of water: he turneth it withersoever he will." So the plans of God for the future are often prophesied in great detail. For example, we are plainly told in Daniel 9:25 that Christ was to be born 483 years (69 weeks of years) from the going forth of the command to rebuild Jerusalem in the days of Ezra and Nehemiah. Christ

was to be born of a virgin (Isa. 7:14). He was to be born in
Bethlehem (Mic. 5:2). He was to be of the house of David
(Isa. 9:6, 7). He must be of the tribe of Judah (Gen. 49:10).
Many details of His crucifixion and the meaning of His
death are told in Psalm 22, Isaiah 53, and elsewhere in Old
Testament prophecy. God does plan ahead in the affairs of
men and works things according to His will.

I. Abraham, Isaac, and Jacob Were Chosen to
Found the Nation Israel

In Genesis 12:1-3 we find how God called out Abraham
to a destiny planned ahead of time for him:

*"Now the Lord had said unto Abram, Get thee out of
thy country, and from thy kindred, and from thy father's
house unto a land that I will shew thee: And I will make of
thee a great nation and I will bless thee, and make thy name
great; and thou shalt be a blessing: And I will bless them
that bless thee, and curse him that curseth thee: and in
thee shall all families of the earth be blessed."*

The promised son was not yet born. Not till the promise
was repeated in various forms did Abraham at last believe
God. In saving faith he committed himself to God (Gen.
15:6). Then was Isaac born.

Note that Abraham was selected for a task, a destiny.
He had the same chance for salvation that every other man
has. He was no more elected to be saved than others are
foreordained to be saved. But he was foreordained to be a
father of many nations, the founder of Israel.

Abraham wished that Ishmael might be chosen as the
one through whom the ancestral line of the nation Israel
and of Christ would run. But God told him no, that the child
of promise, Isaac, would be born of Sarah (Gen. 17:15-21).

God promised many blessings to Ishmael but Isaac was
to be the father of the nation Israel, through whom God
would work out certain great plans.

No hint is given that Ishmael could not be saved the
same as Isaac. The special predestination of Isaac was not
to salvation, but to a certain destiny as father of the Jewish

nation. Ishmael may have been converted or may not have been. At any rate, he could have been saved; that is not the issue here. But to be chosen in destiny as the head of the future Jewish nation was given to Isaac.

Jacob was chosen instead of Esau. As the older twin, Esau had the right of the firstborn to inherit the covenant and promise and the family destiny. But Esau despised that heritage and traded it for a bowl of pottage. How great was Esau's mistake is made clear in Hebrews 12:16, 17:

"Lest there be any fornicator, or profane person, as Esau, who for one morsel of meat sold his birthright. For ye know how that afterwards when he would have inherited the blessing, he was rejected: for he found no place of repentance, though he sought it carefully with tears."

The blessing that Esau did not inherit was the blessing of becoming the father of the Jewish nation, with all the plans God had made for Israel. As far as this destiny was concerned, Esau "found no place of repentance, though he sought it carefully with tears." No reference is made here to the matter of salvation. Esau could have been saved, possibly was saved—we do not know. No one is predestined to be saved or predestined to be lost. On moral matters—matters of right and wrong—every person is allowed to choose for himself. But God settled that Jacob should inherit the promises God had made to Abraham and Isaac, and Esau later could not repent and take back the birthright he had despised.

God had known ahead of time about Jacob and Esau, and had made a choice. God had told Rebekah before the twins were born, "Two nations are in thy womb, and two manner of people shall be separated from thy bowels; and the one people shall be stronger than the other people; and the elder shall serve the younger" (Gen. 25:23).

The New Testament refers to this Scripture and this truth in the following language:

"And not only this; but when Rebecca also had conceived by one, even by our father Isaac; (For the children being not yet born, neither having done any good or evil,

that the purpose of God according to election might stand, not of works, but of him that calleth;) It was said unto her, The elder shall serve the younger. As it is written, Jacob have I loved, but Esau have I hated."—Rom. 9:10-13.

The quotation, "Jacob have I loved, but Esau have I hated," is from Malachi 1:1-3. There we find that the loving and hating were not for the individuals Jacob and Esau so much as for the two nations represented. ". . . Was not Esau Jacob's brother? saith the Lord: yet I loved Jacob, And I hated Esau, and laid his mountains and his heritage waste for the dragons of the wilderness."

God had chosen the nation Israel, of which Jacob was the father, for certain national destiny. And between Edom, the country populated by the descendants of Esau, and Israel, God had chosen Israel and rejected Edom.

Again, we should take pains to note that nothing is said here to indicate that God would save a Jew quicker than He would save an Edomite, a descendant from Esau. That is not the meaning of the passage at all. Concerning salvation we are plainly told, "God is no respecter of persons" (Acts 10:34). But for a nation through which the Scriptures would be given and the Redeemer would come, God chose Jacob and his descendants and rejected Esau and his descendants.

II. In a Special Sense, Israel Is a Chosen People and Nation

God said to Abraham about Isaac, ". . . and I will establish my covenant with him for an everlasting covenant, and with his seed after him" (Gen. 17:19). Later God told Jacob, ". . . fear not to go down into Egypt; for I will there make of thee a great nation," and that He would bring the nation out of Egypt (Gen. 46:3, 4).

After the exodus, God instructed Moses to tell the people, "Now therefore, if ye will obey my voice indeed, and keep my covenant, then ye shall be a peculiar treasure unto me above all people: for all the earth is mine: And ye shall be unto me a kingdom of priests, and an holy nation. These are the words which thou shalt speak unto the chil-

dren of Israel" (Exod. 19:5, 6). Israel, then, is "an holy nation," that is, a set-apart people. So in Isaiah 45:4 God
speaks of "Jacob my servant's sake, and Israel mine elect
. . . ." And again in Isaiah 65:9, 22, Israel is called of God,
"mine elect."

This great distinction for Israel is recognized in Romans 9:4, 5:

*"Who are Israelites; to whom pertaineth the adoption,
and the glory, and the covenants, and the giving of the law,
and the service of God, and the promises; Whose are the
fathers, and of whom as concerning the flesh Christ came,
who is over all God blessed for ever. Amen."*

God had great plans for Israel the nation, and through
Israel came the Old Testament with its priesthood, cere-
monies, and figures; from Israel came the prophets, and at
last the Lord Jesus Christ.

However, in the same Scripture it is made clear that
this election, this choosing of Israel, did not mean salvation
for every Jew. "That is, They which are the children of the
flesh, these are not the children of God: but the children of
the promise are counted for the seed" (Rom. 9:8).

The same thing is taught in Romans 4:13, "For the
promise, that he should be the heir of the world, was not to
Abraham, or to his seed, through the law, but through the
righteousness of faith."

A Jew is saved only by faith. A Jew who does not per-
sonally trust Christ for salvation will not take part in the
kingdom of Christ on earth and will not inherit the great
promises of Abraham.

Of the elect nation we are told, "Esaias also crieth concerning Israel, Though the number of the children of Israel
be as the sand of the sea, a remnant shall be saved" (Rom.
9:27).

But "God hath not cast away his people which he foreknew" but "there is a remnant according to the election of
grace" (Rom. 11:1-6).

In Matthew 24:31 Jesus tells of the time when He will
regather the nation Israel to Palestine when He Himself re-

turns to sit on David's throne and reign. This saved remnant of Israel is called the elect. He said, ". . . he shall send his angels with a great sound of a trumphet, and they shall gather together his elect from the four winds, from one end of heaven to the other."

The Lord Jesus told Nicodemus, a ruler of the Jews, "Except a man be born again, he cannot see the kingdom of God." And when Christ comes to reign on the earth, not a single Jew will enter that kingdom, nor a Gentile, except those who have been born again, just as now, in the spiritual kingdom of God, one cannot enter without the new birth, personal faith in Christ.

III. God Chose Ahead of Time Other Individuals, and Predestined Them to Particular Work for Him

We have seen how God selected Abraham, Isaac, and Jacob for the work of founding the nation Israel. According to the Scriptures, a good many other individuals were selected of God ahead of time to do certain works.

For example, David was chosen to be the second king of Israel. But he was chosen also to found a dynasty that should never die, but would come to its great climax in the Lord Jesus Christ who should eventually restore David's throne and sit upon it. That is clearly taught in Psalm 89:19-37 and in II Samuel 7:8-17. A similar record of that great covenant with David is given in I Chronicles 17:7-15.

In I Kings 13:2 it was foretold that of the house of David, God would raise up a king, Josiah by name, who would offer the idolatrous priests on Jeroboam's false altar. And this came to pass more than three hundred years later (II Kings 23:15-20). God knew ahead of time that He would lead Josiah to defile and destroy the false altar.

You will note that this is not predestination to salvation. God knew that Josiah would be saved, of course, but he was not compelled to be saved. That is not the point of election and predestination. God chose Josiah ahead of time to do a certain work for Him.

In Isaiah 44:28 and 45:1 Cyrus, the great king, is

named over two hundred years ahead of time as one who would order the restoration of Jerusalem and the temple, and this was before the temple was destroyed and the people were carried captive!

It is quite clear also from a number of Scriptures that God selected Nebuchadnezzar for the work which he would do.

IV. Pharaoh Raised Up as an Example of God's Wrath

The case of Pharaoh has troubled many Christians. Seventeen times in the book of Exodus it is said either that "God hardened Pharaoh's heart," or "Pharaoh hardened his heart," or "Pharaoh's heart was hardened."

However, it is a mistake to suppose that God made Pharaoh's heart hard about the matter of salvation. No, after Pharaoh had long gone on in sin, after he had rejected every offer of mercy, God caused and allowed Pharaoh to have a stubborn heart, so that he insisted on keeping the Hebrew people in slavery in Egypt. His heart was hardened on that matter so that God could make him an example of the destruction that comes on people who resist God.

Pharaoh could have been saved. All his murderous persecution of Israel showed that he did not want to be saved. His rejection of the signs and the messages from God brought by Moses shows he did not love God, that he did not repent of his sins, that he did not seek to be saved. God hardened Pharaoh's heart in the sense that when Pharaoh was stubborn, God pressed the matter to a conclusion and made an example of this rebellious sinner.

That matter is brought up again in the New Testament. In Romans 9, where God speaks of how He had planned ahead of time to use the nation Israel, verses 17-24 have the following to say about Pharaoh and about how God deals with stubborn and wicked hearts:

"For the scripture saith unto Pharaoh, Even for this same purpose have I raised thee up, that I might shew my power in thee, and that my name might be declared throughout all the earth. Therefore hath he mercy on whom

he will have mercy, and whom he will he hardeneth. Thou wilt say then unto me, Why doth he yet find fault? For who hath resisted his will? Nay but, O man, who art thou that repliest against God? Shall the thing formed say to him that formed it, Why hast thou made me thus? Hath not the potter power over the clay of the same lump to make one vessel unto honour, and another unto dishonour? What if God, willing to shew his wrath, and to make his power known endured with much longsuffering the vessels of wrath fitted to destruction: And that he might make known the riches of his glory on the vessels of mercy, which he had afore prepared unto glory. Even us, whom he hath called, not of the Jews only, but also of the Gentiles?"

Note here that the mercy mentioned in verse 18 is not the mercy of salvation which is offered to everyone alike. But it was the mercy that God shows to wicked sinners for so long, even when they will not be saved. Of course, that mercy may be withdrawn and God may bring them to judgment as always, in this life or the next, He does. That mercy is the "much longsuffering" mentioned in verse 22 which God endures toward "the vessels of wrath fitted to destruction."

Pharaoh was a vessel suitable for God's wrath. He was "fitted to destruction." He was an enemy of God, an enemy of the people of God. Often warned, he would not repent. Must we blame God that the divine rule laid down in Proverbs 29:1 came to pass, "He, that being often reproved hardeneth his neck, shall suddenly be destroyed, and that without remedy"?

Since Pharaoh did not love God, would not serve God, would not obey Him, would not turn from his sins, then God brought an issue where the wicked man must make an open choice. That issue was God's demand to let Israel go. So Pharaoh hardened his heart. It is true that, since God pressed the issue, God hardened his heart. It is also true that "Pharaoh's heart was hardened," that is, as a result of his long sin, and the chain of circumstances, inevitably his heart was hardened.

But knowing the wickedness of this man, God raised him up to show God's power and for the glory of God and the good of men. "For the scripture saith unto Pharaoh, Even for this same purpose have I raised thee up, that I might shew my power in thee, and that my name might be declared throughout all the earth" (Rom. 9:17).

Every lost sinner who rejects God's offer of mercy, who turns down the Saviour, who refuses to repent of his sins, will eventually stand before Christ at the great white throne judgment. God will there make a public example of that sinner. There the books will be opened and he will be judged out of the things written in the books according to his works. And there God Himself will be vindicated. Every person who ever lived, every angel, every devil, will see that God has done right in letting the wicked, Christ-rejecting sinner go to Hell for his sins when he would not accept the offer of mercy.

But God so used Pharaoh before his death. It seems obvious that Pharaoh had already settled himself and crystallized his will against God. He had chosen: should he continue his murderous enslavement of God's people or release them? Right or wrong, he would continue. He would reject the true God. He would not repent. We believe he had already committed the unpardonable sin. So God made him stubborn in the matter of the release of the children of Israel from bondage, and made him a public example of God's wrath. Really, God did this in lovingkindness to all who would hear, "that he might make known the riches of his glory on the vessels of mercy, which he had afore prepared unto glory, Even us . . ." as Romans 9:23, 24 tell us.

God did raise up Pharaoh for destruction, and had him drowned in the Red Sea. But God did not predestinate Pharaoh to be lost. He was a wicked sinner who would not be moved by God's mercy, nor by the message of God's servant, nor the mighty signs which were shown him. He was already an impenitent sinner, so God made an example of Pharaoh. And God doubtless does the same thing today with many a man who dies violently, after years of sin. So, doubtless, it was with Hitler and with Mussolini. But either of them could have been saved if in his heart he had repented and turned to Christ in faith. Since they went long in stubborn sin and wickedness, it was proper and right that these vessels of wrath fitted to destruction should be made a public example of the judgment of God on such sinners.

Chapter IV

Christ's Atoning Death Paid for the Sins of Every Person Ever Born

It is only by ignoring a great mass of Scriptures and many, many explicit statements in the Word of God that anyone can think that salvation is provided only for a few. From one end to the other, the Scriptures teach that God has provided salvation for everyone who would ever live and that whosoever will may be saved.

God has plainly told us that Christ atoned for the sins of the whole world, that God's tender heart longs to see all saved, that light and invitation and conviction does come to every sinner, and that the blessed invitation is given to every son and daughter of Adam to repent and trust Christ for salvation!

That proof is so abundant and so unanswerable that I hope the reader will take it much to heart. Only by refusing to hear what God says can one say God *is* willing for any to be lost.

I. Jesus Is the "Saviour of the World," Not of a Selected Few

The Samaritan men who heard the testimony of the woman of Sychar and then came and heard the Lord Jesus for themselves said, ". . . this is indeed the Christ, the Sav-

iour of the world" (John 4:42). Is Christ really "the Saviour
of the world," and not just Saviour of a part of the world?
Yes, Christ is potentially the Saviour of the whole world. In
I John 4:14 He is given that title again, "And we have seen
and do testify that the Father sent the Son to be the Saviour
of the world." Not every person in the world takes Christ as
his Saviour, but that is what the Father sent the Son for—
to be the Saviour of the world.

The Apostle Paul tells why he labors so hard to
get everybody to trust the Saviour: "For therefore we
both labour and suffer reproach, because we trust in the living God, who is the Saviour of all men, specially of those
that believe" (I Tim. 4:10).

Paul wanted everybody to hear the Gospel, because
Christ is "the Saviour of all men, specially of those that believe." He is, in general, a Saviour of all men. He is, especially and particularly, only a Saviour of those who trust Him.
But that is the fault of men, not the fault of God. Christ
came to pay for the sins of the world and offer Himself as
a Saviour to every man.

Is not that same thing taught in John 3:16, 17?

*"For God so loved the world, that he gave his only be-
gotten Son, that whosoever believeth in him should not perish, but have everlasting life. For God sent not his Son into
the world to condemn the world; but that the world through
him might be saved."*

It is the whole world that God loves. It is the whole
world for which Christ died! And God did not send His
Son into the world to condemn the world, nor any part of it,
but He sent His Son "that the world through him might be
saved."

This is restated in the Bible so many times that to try
to evade the truth that Christ died for all men seems im-
moral, seems to show some prejudice and bias against the
Bible at face value.

In John 12:47 Jesus said:

"And if any man hear my words, and believe not, I

judge him not: for I came not to judge the world, but to save the world."

What did Jesus come for? "I came not to judge the world, but to save the world," Jesus said. He wanted to save not a few individuals, but the world. Any person who without bias takes the Scripture at face value, is bound to believe that the Lord Jesus wanted to save the whole world, and died for the sins of the world.

It is true that all who reject the Saviour are damned and ought to be damned. But it is still mercifully true that salvation has been purchased on the cross for every sinner.

The first epistle of John is written primarily to Christians. And John writes to teach Christians how to have joy and fellowship with God the Father and with the Son. He says, "My little children, these things write I unto you, that ye sin not. And if any man sin, we have an advocate with the Father, Jesus Christ the righteous" (I John 2:1). Oh, blessed be God, we poor, failing, sinning Christians have an advocate with the Father, Jesus Christ the righteous! One who has been saved can day by day confess and forsake his sins and have cleansing anew, and fellowship with the Father and the Son.

But the Holy Spirit did not allow John to leave the matter there. The next verse continues, "And he is the propitiation for our sins: and not for our's only, but also for the sins of the whole world." You see, it is a blessed truth that Christ is the advocate for Christians and that all of our sins are paid for. It is a blessed truth that we can come day by day for the new cleansing and the renewed fellowship which we so often need. But God does not want this blessed truth to obscure the greater fact—Christ is the propitiation FOR THE SINS OF THE WHOLE WORLD! Every person ever born had his sins paid for. He could have had them forgiven if he would. He could have been a child of God if he would. The atonement of Jesus Christ on the cross paid for the sins of every poor sinner ever born! No reader can look up to the bleeding Saviour on the cross and then say that God intended that reader to go to Hell! His sins are paid for; he could be saved and ought to be saved!

II. The "INIQUITY OF US ALL" Laid on Jesus

What kind of atonement is pictured in Isaiah 53, that gospel chapter in the Old Testament? There we are told that Jesus was "despised and rejected of men; a man of sorrows, and acquainted with grief." There we are told, "Surely he hath borne our griefs, and carried our sorrows." There we are told, "But he was wounded for our transgressions, he was bruised for our iniquities: the chastisement of our peace was upon him; and with his stripes we are healed." Isaiah, this silver-tongued evangelist of the Old Testament, knew that Jesus died for sinners. But how many sinners? Did He die for all or for only a minority of men? Was it an atonement and propitiation for all men everywhere or for only a selected few?

Isaiah 53:6 tells us plainly, "All we like sheep have gone astray; we have turned every one to his own way: and the Lord hath laid on him the iniquity of us all."

How many have gone astray? "All . . . have gone astray."

How have we sinned? "We have turned every one to his own way."

How much of the iniquity of mankind was laid on Jesus?

"The Lord hath laid on him THE INIQUITY OF US ALL."

If words have any meaning, then the iniquity of the whole sinning human race was laid on Jesus Christ. If "all" in the first of verse six means all human kind have sinned, then "all" in the last of verse six means that all have their sins paid for, and that all may be forgiven!

A famous English preacher preached in an English town and then rushed to catch a train for London.

A sinner heard the preacher, became deeply convicted, and felt he must settle now the matter of salvation. So he followed the preacher to the train and just as the train pulled into the station he seized the preacher's lapel and with anxious heart and voice inquired, "But I want to be saved. I must be saved! Tell me how!"

The minister said, "I must catch this last train to London. Do you have a Bible?"

"Yes, I have one at home," said the anxious inquirer.

"Then find Isaiah 53:6," said the minister. "Listen very carefully. In Isaiah 53:6 go in at the first 'all' and come out at the last 'all' and you will be saved."

The preacher was hustled into the train and the inquirer left alone. He went back to his home and in the Bible sought Isaiah 53:6. "What did he mean?" he mused. "Go in at the first 'all' and come out at the last 'all' of Isaiah 53: 6 and you will be saved."

He found the verse and read it carefully. "All we like sheep have gone astray." "Well," he said to himself, "I can certainly go in at the first 'all.' I have gone astray like a lost sheep. I am a poor lost sinner!"

And then he read the last part of the verse, "And the Lord hath laid on him the iniquity of us all." And he said to himself, "Then if I come out at the last 'all,' I must believe that Jesus took my place, paid for my sins, and that all my iniquities are paid for on the cross. And if I rely upon that, I will be saved, the minister said!"

So he trusted Christ and was saved. He trusted the Saviour who bore the iniquity of us ALL.

This same blessed truth, that Christ paid for the sins of all sinners everywhere, is taught in Hebrews 2:9. Read this blessed Scripture and believe it and rejoice:

"But we see Jesus, who was made a little lower than the angels for the suffering of death, crowned with glory and honour; that he by the grace of God should taste death for every man."

The dear Lord Jesus came into this world for the suffering of death and He did it, "that he by the grace of God should taste death FOR EVERY MAN."

Jesus died not for a few but for all, literally for every man.

Would it not be wicked to doubt or to try to explain away such explicit statements in the Word of God? We may say simply that the so-called "limited atonement" is not mentioned in the Bible and is not taught in the Bible. For

God arranged that every person who should ever live could be saved if he would.

In I Timothy 2:5, 6 the same blessed doctrine is explicitly stated: "For there is one God, and one mediator between God and men, the man Christ Jesus; WHO GAVE HIMSELF A RANSOM FOR ALL. . . ."

How could language be plainer? Any honest Christian who takes the Bible at face value must accept it that the Lord Jesus Christ gave Himself a ransom for all, that is, for every sinner ever born! So the Bible plainly says and so Bible believers must believe.

III. The Bible Pictures an Atonement as Universal as Sin

There rises in my heart a holy indignation when I face that man-made term "limited atonement," for that term is exact opposite of what the Bible teaches.

Men, speaking not by the authority of God's Word, but by human wisdom and philosophy, following Augustine or Calvin, say that if Christ died for some sinner who is never saved, then God's love and grace were thwarted. And so to insist on a man-made doctrine of "absolute sovereignty of God," by which they mean that God never offered anybody anything that He did not compel them to take, they make God the author and planner of every sin that ever occurred! They even say that God Himself planned for Adam to sin, because they do not want to allow that God's love could be rejected and God's grace refused.

But the simple truth is that nearly everybody who was ever saved first heard the Gospel many times and was called many times before he answered. When I was saved at about nine years of age, God's blessed Spirit had been after me, convicting me, for at least five years! Men are called who do not come. And God purchased salvation for all, whether they receive it or not.

In the book of Romans, the great epistle written on the theme of the grace of God, we find again and again this blessed teaching that God's loving atonement for sin went as far as sin went and beyond, that the grace of salvation is as universally offered and provided for as man's sin.

In Romans 3:9-20 we have a terrible indictment of the whole human race. There are fourteen charges against mankind, all of mankind. And note how universal is God's charge:

"They are all under sin" (vs. 9).

"There is none righteous, no, not one" (vs. 10).

"There is none that understandeth, there is none that seeketh after God" (vs. 11).

"They are all gone out of the way . . . there is none that doeth good, no, not one" (vs. 12).

"That every mouth may be stopped, and all the world may become guilty before God" (vs. 19).

"For there is no difference: For all have sinned, and come short of the glory of God" (vss. 22, 23).

Here we clearly see that sin has marked and damned every person ever born.

And now follows the blessed teaching that if all have sinned, all may be freely justified.

Now read this passage with this in mind: "For there is no difference: For all have sinned, and come short of the glory of God: Being justified freely by his grace through the redemption that is in Christ Jesus."

Would not any humble, honest Christian reading that properly understand that it is those who have sinned who may be freely justified? Of course in verse 22 we are told that this is "the righteousness of God which is by faith of Jesus Christ unto all and upon all them that believe." We are not speaking of any salvation that does not depend on the righteousness of Christ and His atonement for our sins. But does not that Scripture properly infer that as all have sinned, all may be freely justified?

But let us go further. In verses 22 and 23 the Scripture says, "For there is no difference: For all have sinned and come short of the glory of God." Now in the same epistle, in Romans 10:12, the same blessed Holy Spirit says, "For there is no difference between the Jew and the Greek: for the same Lord over all is rich unto all that call upon him."

There is no difference, for all have sinned. There is no difference, all may be saved.

Jesus Christ is the "same Lord over all." He is not one kind of a Lord to those predestined to be saved and another kind of Lord to those who are predestined to be lost. As far as atoning for their sins and making a way of salvation is concerned, Jesus Christ is the same Lord over all, over Jews and over Gentiles. If "there is no difference" means that all have sinned, then the same term, talking about salvation, "there is no difference," means that all may be saved.

But this is not an isolated instance. In the book of Romans this teaching appears many times. In Romans, chapter 5, it is so emphatic and clear that one dare not twist it to mean anything else.

There verse 18 says, "Therefore as by the offence of one judgment came upon all men to condemnation; even so by the righteousness of one the free gift came upon all men unto justification of life."

Here is the blessed teaching. The first Adam sinned and so the whole human race became sinners. The second Adam died and paid for sin so "the free gift came upon all men unto justification of life."

The clear teaching here is that as far as the offense went, the atonement went. As many men as became sinners by Adam's fall—that many were provided for in Christ's atoning death! Any other interpretation of the Scripture would be a biased and less than honest interpretation.

Again in Romans 5:20 the Scripture says, "Moreover the law entered, that the offence might abound. But where sin abounded, grace did much more abound." Here is the clear rule: "But where sin abounded, grace did much more abound." To say that grace does not reach as far as sin reaches would be a denial of the plain statement of God. No, the Bible teaches an atonement which is no more limited than sin is limited, "Where sin abounded, grace did much more abound."

The sixth chapter of Romans carries out this theme and verse 23 sums it up again: "For the wages of sin is death; but the gift of God is eternal life through Jesus Christ our Lord." There is no hint that the wages of sin is death for only part of mankind. This is true universally. So it is fair to understand the tenor of Scriptures as teaching that the gift of God is eternal life for those who have sinned, if they will but have it.

In Romans 8:32 this contrast of universal sin balanced by universal atonement is stated again: "He that spared not his own Son, but delivered him up for us all, how shall he not with him also freely give us all things?"

God did not spare His beloved Son Jesus, "but delivered him up FOR US ALL." The atonement is for all. However far sin went to damn the whole human race, the righteousness of God went further in Christ, God's sacrifice for sins! Here is no talk of a man-made philosophy of a limited atonement, but here is the clear teaching that God gave up His Son FOR US ALL.

God says of Jews and Gentiles, "For God hath concluded them all in unbelief, that he might have mercy upon all" (Rom. 11:32). How many have been condemned in unbelief? The answer is, "For God hath concluded THEM ALL in unbelief." And how many are included in the mercy of God? The answer is, "That he might have mercy UPON ALL."

I am saying that throughout the book of Romans, and in many other places in the Bible, the grace of God is made as extensive as the fact of man's sin.

In fact, that is the teaching of Isaiah 53:6. "All we like sheep have gone astray . . . and the Lord hath laid on him the iniquity of us all." Where sin abounded, grace did much more abound.

The same balance, that the grace of God and His atoning provision for man's salvation are coextensive with the fact of sin and as universally provided for man as sin has cursed man, is taught in I Corinthians 15:21, 22.

"For since by man came death, by man came also the resurrection of the dead. For as in Adam all die, even so in Christ shall all be made alive."

This Scripture plainly teaches that as all men potentially became sinners by Adam's sin, so all that are ever born are potentially made alive in Christ.

That means that no one ever went to Hell because of Adam's sin. Whatever was lost in Adam was regained in Christ!

These verses teach that little unaccountable children, infants who never knew right from wrong, who never consciously accepted or rejected Christ, are kept safe by the blood of Christ until they come to know and choose for themselves right or wrong, and become consciously sinners.

Read that passage again and see that just as universally "as in Adam all die," just as universally "so in Christ shall all be made alive." In both cases the death and salvation are potential, for the race of sinners was not yet born when Adam sinned, but his sin potentially made all sinners. And so although some have not trusted Christ for salvation, He is the Saviour of the world, and potentially the Saviour of all, depending on their faith in Him.

These Scriptures make absurd the Calvinistic invention of a "limited atonement." No, Jesus Christ died for the sins of the whole world, and all may be saved if they will.

Chapter V

God's Love, Enlightenment, Enabling and Invitation Reach Every Sinner

Not only did Christ atone for every man's sin. His love reaches all, His Spirit enlightens every heart, His enabling grace goes with His command for all to repent, and in the Bible He clearly invites all to be saved. No one need go to Hell. Provision is made so every sinner can be saved.

I. The Loving Heart of God Longs to See All People Saved

What is God's attitude toward sinners? Does He pick and choose among them, so that this one He loves and this one He hates, this one He wants to save and this one He has no concern for? Is that God's attitude toward sinners? Is that the attitude of the Lord Jesus toward sinners? Thank God, we know from the Bible that it is not! God's loving heart has deep concern for every lost sinner and God wants men, all men everywhere, to be saved.

How plainly and how often the Scripture reminds us of this! In II Peter 3:9 we are told, "The Lord is not slack concerning his promise, as some men count slackness; but is longsuffering to usward, not willing that any should perish, but that all should come to repentance."

God is not willing that any should perish! God wants all to come to repentance.

In I Timothy 2:3, 4, this is stated again. There we are told, "For this is good and acceptable in the sight of God our Saviour; Who will have all men to be saved, and to come unto the knowledge of the truth."

God "will have all men to be saved." God wants all "to come unto the knowledge of the truth," and that, the following verses explain, is why Christ died as a ransom for all.

It was the whole world that "God so loved . . . that he gave his only begotten Son." It was the heart's desire and the holy, loving concern of God that every person in the world should be saved—not to condemn the world, but that the world through Him might be saved.

Again, that love of God for every person and His concern that all might be saved is expressed in the inspired words of Acts 17:30. There Paul is recorded as speaking to the Athenians as follows, "And the times of this ignorance God winked at; but now commandeth all men every where to repent."

God wants "all men every where to repent."

No one has a right to blame God if he goes to Hell! Any foolish preacher who makes it appear that God is not willing to save some people sins against the Gospel, sins against the loving heart of God, and perverts the Scriptures.

II. God Has Given Light and Witness and Holy Spirit Conviction to Every Sinner So That All Could Be Saved

Hyper-Calvinists often say that a sinner cannot repent without the enabling grace of God. That is true, but every sinner does have the enabling grace of God. Every sinner has some light from God. Every sinner has some witness, some conviction from God.

It is true as Jesus said, "A man can receive nothing, except it be given him from heaven" (John 3:27). It is true as Jesus said again, "No man can come to me, except the Father which hath sent me draw him . . . (John 6:44). But those who conclude, therefore, that some people cannot be saved, are mistaken. They forget the many times we are told that God deals with every sinner, draws every sinner.

When Jesus was lifted up on the cross, He set in motion powers, appeals, and movings of the Holy Spirit which would reach every person ever born. For He Himself said in John 12:32, 33, "And I, if I be lifted up from the earth, will draw all men unto me. This he said, signifying what death he should die." He was so lifted up on the cross; so He does draw all men unto Him!

The same truth is given in the first chapter of John. Verse 4 says, "In him was life; and the life was the light of men." He was not the light of only some men, but the light of men, of all men.

In verse 7 we are told, "The same came for a witness, to bear witness of the Light, that all men through him might believe." The plan was "that all men through him might believe."

In verse 9 we are told more positively yet, "That was the true Light, which lighteth every man that cometh into the world." Every person who ever came into the world has felt the pull of Christ, felt some light from Christ.

Do you wonder at that? Then remember, "The heavens declare the glory of God; and the firmament sheweth his handywork. Day unto day uttereth speech, and night unto night sheweth knowledge. There is no speech nor language, where their voice is not heard" (Ps. 19:1-3).

At Lystra Paul and Barnabas told the people who worshiped idols of the living and true God who made all things. They said, "Nevertheless he left not himself without witness, in that he did good, and gave us rain from heaven, and fruitful seasons, filling our hearts with food and gladness" (Acts 14:17). The people at Lystra had a message from God before Paul and Barnabas preached the Gospel to them.

When God calls all men to judgment, as He will, every man will find that he will be held accountable for certain light, certain knowledge, certain invitations which he experienced. In Romans 2:14-16 we are told how those who do not have the Scriptures have the law of God written in their hearts, attested by their conscience, holding them accountable for their continuance in sin and their rejection of Christ. Read it here:

"For when the Gentiles, which have not the law, do by nature the things contained in the law, these, having not the law, are a law unto themselves: Which shew the work of the law written in their hearts, their conscience also bearing witness, and their thoughts the mean while accusing or else excusing one another;) In the day when God shall judge the secrets of men by Jesus Christ according to my gospel."

You see, God has put a witness in the hearts of all men showing that they are sinners. Heathen people who have gone on in sin have sometimes been turned over to their reprobate minds. Yet, without the Scriptures, they still have a conscience which warns them of their sin and their need for God. They still have daily witness that there is a Creator whom they ought to seek. They still have witness that there is some benevolent, loving God who wishes them well.

We have a remarkable example of a heathen man who, without the Scriptures and without preaching, sought God. That man was Cornelius who, according to the tenth chapter of Acts, "feared God with all his house, which gave much alms to the people, and prayed to God alway" (vs. 2). This man followed what light he had; he prayed to God, he gave to the poor, he tried to do right. Such a poor sinner who followed what light he had must be given more light. So God sent an angel to tell him where he could find Peter who would tell him words "whereby thou and all thy house shall be saved" (Acts 11:14). As far as I know, Cornelius had no Bible, no Old Testament Scriptures; yet with what light he had, he sought God. As far as we know, he had never heard the preaching of the Word; yet he had witness, he had conviction, he had light from God. And God will give further light to every man who follows the light he has. Men do not go to Hell because they never heard the Gospel; they go to Hell because they are sinners, sinners who do not follow what light they do have.

The blessed Holy Spirit is in the world to bring conviction to sinners. We may not always know how and when the blessed Holy Spirit convicts sinners but He does, in some measure and in some method, convict all lost people. For in John 16:8 Jesus told the disciples about the Comforter whom He would send, and said, "And when he is come, he will reprove the world of sin, and of righteousness and of judgment.

God who, in the Bible, commanded all men to repent, has carried that reproof to the hearts of sinners of the whole world through the Holy Spirit. Christ who died for the world has, by His crucifixion, drawn all men, whether they come to Him or not. Christ is that true Light "which lighteth every man that cometh into the world" (John 1:9).

In fact, when Zacharias, the father of John the Baptist, was filled with the Holy Ghost after the birth of his promised son John, he praised God and said that Christ had come to save His people "through the tender mercy of our God; whereby the dayspring from on high hath visited us, To give light to them that sit in darkness and in the shadow of death, to guide our feet into the way of peace" (Luke 1:78, 79).

III. Dead Sinners Can Repent Because Christ's Command Assures His Enabling

I heard a hyper-Calvinist a few weeks ago, a famous man, say, "Why tell people to repent who cannot repent?

A man cannot repent until he has been regenerated. A lost sinner is dead, and he can do nothing until God makes him alive."

It is true that in a spiritual sense every lost sinner is dead, that is, he does not have everlasting life, the life of salvation. But in the sense of being accountable for his sins, knowing about his sins, having the freedom to choose for God or the Devil, men are not dead. Their minds, their consciences, their powers of choice are not dead. They are dead in trespasses and in sins, and so do not have everlasting life in a spiritual sense, but they can choose.

Do you say that a dead man cannot do anything? Well, by human standards and by human power a dead man can do nothing. But when God commands a sinner to repent, he can repent. And the Scripture plainly says beyond any argument that He is ". . . not willing that any should perish, but that all should come to repentance" (II Pet. 3:9). Heed it carefully. We have the plain Word of God that "the times of this ignorance God winked at; but now commandeth all men every where to repent" (Acts 17:30). If God commands people to repent, they can. Do you believe God is a crooked God who demands that men repent who cannot repent, and then damns them for not doing what they cannot do?

Can a spiritually dead man repent? Yes, if God tells him to! The truth is that those who are even physically dead will hear the voice of the Lord Jesus and obey Him. For in John 5:28, 29 Jesus said, "Marvel not at this: for the hour is coming, in the which all that are in the graves shall hear his voice, And shall come forth; they that have done good, unto the resurrection of life; and they that have done evil, unto the resurrection of damnation."

When Jesus Christ speaks, a dead man can come out of the grave, whether he is saved or lost! And when Jesus Christ speaks, a man dead in trespasses and in sins can repent and if he does not do so, his eternal ruin will be upon his own head!

Jesus was once in the synagogue on the Sabbath day

before scornful scribes and Pharisees. Present was a man
with a withered hand. We suppose that that drawn and
withered hand could not be manipulated. But Jesus said,
"Stretch forth thy hand. And he did so: and his hand was
restored whole as the other" (Luke 6:10). A man whose
hand is withered can do anything with it Jesus Christ tells
him to do.

Peter, in the name of Christ, took hold of the hand of a
lame man who from the day of his birth had never walked
and said, "In the name of Jesus Christ of Nazareth rise up
and walk" (Acts 3:6). And the man who could not walk, yet
obeyed, rose, walked, leaped, and praised God! You see, when
God gives an order, He gives the power to obey that order.
When God commands people to repent, He makes it possible
for them to repent. Those who are spiritually dead can hear
the voice of the Son of God, and when He commands them
to repent, they can repent. For God's Holy Spirit is present
to convict, to enlighten, to enable the will.

IV. God Gives Blessed Invitations to All to Come and Be Saved

This Bible is full of blessed invitations. All the way
from the time in the Garden of Eden when a brokenhearted
God runs after Adam calling for him, down to the final
promise in the last chapter of the last book in the Bible,
God invites people to come and be saved.

How many are the all-inclusive invitations in the Bible!
Listen to that Old Testament evangelist, Isaiah: "Look
unto me, and be ye saved, all the ends of the earth: for I
am God, and there is none else" (Isa. 45:22). Here Isaiah
gives God's blessed invitation to "all the ends of the earth"
and he follows that invitation to "all the ends of the earth"
with a solemn warning that "unto me every knee shall bow,
every tongue shall swear." If God's Word means what it
says, may not all the ends of the earth come and be saved?

Again Isaiah pleads, "Ho, every one that thirsteth,
come ye to the waters, and he that hath no money; come
ye, buy, and eat; yea, come, buy wine and milk without
money and without price" (Isa. 55:1).

To whom is this sweet invitation? It is to "every one that thirsteth." There is spiritual wine and milk without money and without price. Everyone may come and buy what Christ has already paid for and may eat to the full because the invitation is to "every one that thirsteth."

In the same chapter the Scripture says, "Let the wicked forsake his way, and the unrighteous man his thoughts: and let him return unto the Lord, and he will have mercy upon him; and to our God, for he will abundantly pardon" (Isa. 55:7).

Who here is invited? "The wicked." And who is it that should forsake his thoughts and plans and return to the Lord for mercy? It is "the unrighteous man." Not some few selected persons, not a restricted tribe or race or group, but the wicked and unrighteous are all invited to turn for mercy and pardon!

Joel gives the blessed promise, "And it shall come to pass, that whosoever shall call on the name of the Lord shall be delivered" (Joel 2:32). And that blessed promise, "Whosoever shall call on the name of the Lord shall be saved," is repeated twice in the New Testament. It once was given at Pentecost in Acts 2:21. It is repeated again in Romans 10:13, "For whosoever shall call upon the name of the Lord shall be saved."

What a wonderful word is this "whosoever." How blessed that it starts in the Old Testament, that it is repeated in the book of Acts, then repeated again in the book of Romans! Three times God says it, that "whosoever shall call upon the name of the Lord shall be saved."

That "whosoever" must mean whosoever. Anyone can be saved.

In the mind of the Spirit I see an old man, the Apostle John, some ninety years old and more, on the Isle of Patmos, an exile for the faith. And the resurrected Saviour meets John and gives him the messages to the seven churches of Asia Minor. John is commanded to write the words that will close the canon of Scripture. After this no one may add to these words nor take from these words without terrible penalties. But God says to the old saint with a quill pen in his hand, "Wait, John! We must not close the canon of Scripture without another sweet, blessed invitation to sinners."

The aged John stills the trembling fingers of his withered old hand and says, "What shall I write then, Lord Jesus?"

Jesus answered back, "Write it again, that 'the Spirit and the bride say, Come. And let him that heareth say, Come. And let him that is athirst come. And whosoever will, let him take the water of life freely'" (Rev. 22:17).

The blessed Holy Spirit says, "Come." From the context we know that the Spirit addresses this word to every person in the world. And everybody who hears it ought to repeat it and say, "Come." And everyone who is thirsty ought to come. And whosoever will, that is, literally everyone who is willing, may take the water of life freely.

Some people think that God gave all these blessed invitations, but that He did not mean just what they say. Of course, they say, everyone is invited but God does not give some people the power to turn to Christ and be saved. They think God has ordained that some should be saved and ordained that others should be lost, and it is only in some figurative and nonliteral sense that all are invited. But what a slanderous reflection that is on the honest intent of God, and what a misrepresentation of the plain language of Scripture!

Some time ago I heard a commercial on television. A company offered a vacuum cleaner for $9.95! It was factory rebuilt, and was a most wonderful bargain! Nothing like this had ever been offered before! But I learned later from others that the offer of a vacuum cleaner for $9.95 was simply a "come-on," not genuinely a bona fide offer. When one responded to the television appeal and wrote for a salesman to bring the vacuum cleaner to the house, it turned out that there had been only a few, and these were already gone. However, he had a much more expensive vacuum cleaner, and of course, very, very, very much better, which he would sell for many times the price of the one advertised!

In some cases the salesman actually brought an old machine to sell for $9.95, but he frankly told the people it was not worth the price, it was used and did not have the necessary attachments, etc. He strongly advised them to buy the more expensive machine, and he happened to have one with him! I learned in these cases the very attractive offer was made simply to get contacts with people to whom the salesman expected to sell a much more expensive machine.

Does any reader think that the dear God who gave His Son to die on Calvary practices that kind of salesmanship? Do you believe that God said "whosoever will, let him take the water of life freely," but that He had already made it so many could not choose to be saved? Do you believe that God thus uses language which, to all sensible people, appears to be addressed to everybody, but that secretly He meant it only for a selected few, and that the others He had consigned, before they were born, to the fires of Hell? What a shocking attitude to have toward the wonderfully sweet, pure words of the Lord Jesus!

No, no, this is no "come-on"; this is no selling "gimmick." These blessed invitations are the pure Word of God. God means what He says. Whosoever will may come. The fact that God says "whosoever" means that all can will to come and all must be held accountable if they do not come to Him for mercy and forgiveness and to take the water of life freely.

Some years ago we felt we needed a water softener for our home in Wheaton. One was advertised at a reasonable price. I responded to the ad and a salesman came to call. The water softener which had been advertised so widely and was such a wonderful bargain was really very nice, the salesman said, except that the tank was of ordinary steel. It would rust out in a few months, and he did not advise me to buy it, though, he said, his company made it. But now here, on another circular, he could show me another model with a copper tank which would last indefinitely. Yes, it cost a great deal more, but it was really the best thing for me to buy.

I immediately dismissed the man with scorn. I would listen to no more of his sales talk. It may be that each of the water softeners was worth the money that was asked. But his sales method was insincere and dishonest. I did not choose to deal with that kind of man.

The advertisement had not expressly said that the water softener made of ordinary steel was adequate, but that was the impression given. I do not like to deal with people who make one impression in an advertisement, then when they have a contact and a good prospect of a sale, change their tune and ask for more.

How could I feel toward God, if I should find out that when He said, "whosoever will" He did not mean that, because He had made men so that many of them could not repent if they would? How would I feel toward the Saviour if I found that, though He professed to die for the sins of the whole world, He had already consigned some people to Hell with no chance to repent, no matter how much they wished to do so?

Thank God, the Bible may be taken at face value! We deal with an honest God. The love of God is far greater than the human mind can conceive it. God never overstates His case. When He says, ". . . whosoever will, let him take the water of life freely," He means whosoever will. And when He says that God is "not willing that any should perish, but that all should come to repentance," then we know that His dear, tender heart longs to see every sinner saved. Only those who will not come and be saved are lost.

Chapter VI

Not a Single Soul Is Predestined Without an Opportunity to Be Saved

We have already found from the Word of God that Christ has made atonement for the sins of the whole world, that God loved the whole world, that God was not willing that any should perish, that light and witness and conviction have come to every sinner and that God's blessed invitation is to whosoever will. Surely it is clear by this time that God does not send anybody to Hell without a chance to be saved.

But let us consider the matter further.

I. Not a Single Case Is Ever Mentioned in the Bible Where Anybody Was Predestined to Go to Hell

God's choice of Abraham, Isaac, and Jacob, God's choice of David, of Cyrus, of Nebuchadnezzar, was in every case a choice for a particular service and destiny. No one was appointed to be saved except by the free Gospel which is preached to all alike. No one was ordained to be lost except that they refused to come to Christ. God had only one plan of salvation, and it was offered to all alike.

We are told that Esau was a man who missed out on God's election, and he found no place of repentance though he sought it carefully with tears. But the blessing he missed was the birthright as the father of the nation Israel. It was not a matter of salvation at all. Esau may have been saved or may not have been saved; that is not the matter under discussion. At least he could have been saved. But after he had once scorned the blessed destiny as head of a nation for God, God would not reverse His decision and take the birthright from Jacob to give it to Esau. Esau was not predestined to be lost, and we do not even know whether he was lost or saved.

Pharaoh was raised up that God might show His power. And God hardened Pharaoh, and made him a vessel to dishonor. But again, when God hardened Pharaoh's heart, it was not hardening him against God, against salvation, against the wooing of the Holy Spirit. Pharaoh had already hardened his own heart against God and against the call of mercy. But God made an issue of Pharaoh's rebellion. God pressed the matter of the release of the Israelites to an open break and made a public example of this wicked, murderous man who would not hear the warning of Moses and was not moved by all the signs and wonders that God sent. Pharaoh was not predestined to be lost. I think he *was* lost, but it was because of his own willful rejection of the light and of God's mercy. I think that it was after he had committed the unpardonable sin that God drowned him in the Red Sea. At any rate, Pharaoh was not predestined to go to Hell. He went to Hell after many, many invitations and after deliberate, repeated rejections of God's call and God's mercy. God hardened Pharaoh's heart about letting the children of Israel go free, but Pharaoh had already hardened his heart to continue in sin and rejection.

If there is any one person in history whose wickedness was so great that we might suppose he was predestined to go to Hell, it would be Judas Iscariot. Yet the Bible does not even hint that Judas could not have been saved.

Judas is referred to in Old Testament prophecy several times. Psalm 41:9 speaks of him prophetically as Christ's familiar friend who "lifted up his heel against me" and in John 13:18, 19, Jesus teaches us that that referred to Judas. The betrayal of Christ for thirty pieces of silver is mentioned in Zechariah 11:13. In Acts 1:20 we learn that Psalm 69:25 referred to Judas who lost his place as an apostle by sin. And in John 6:64 we are told that "Jesus knew from the beginning who they were that believed not, and who should betray him." Again, in John 6:70, 71 we learn the following of Judas, "Jesus answered them, Have not I chosen you twelve, and one of you is a devil? He spake of Judas Iscariot the son of Simon: for he it was that should betray him, being one of the twelve."

Then Judas was an unconverted man. The Lord Jesus knew that Judas would betray Him.

And yet there is the lament of a broken heart in Psalm 41:9 about Judas. Here Jesus is pictured as saying, "Yea, mine own familiar friend, in whom I trusted, which did eat of my bread, hath lifted up his heel against me." The dear Lord Jesus loved Judas. He grieved over his betrayal. Judas could have been saved. Even when Judas kissed the cheek of the Saviour in Gethsemane—a signal that they should bind Him and take Him away to trial—Jesus addressed Judas as "Friend" (Matt. 26:50). There is not a hint in the Bible that Judas could not have been saved.

Of course God knows all things. He knew whether Judas would be saved. But the fact that He knew did not please Him. Judas had light from God, as have others. Judas was convicted of his sins, as other sinners have been. Judas would not repent for salvation, but he could have done so. He was not compelled to be lost.

In not a single case in the Bible is it even hinted that any person was foreordained to be lost, that he would not hear the Gospel or have a chance to repent.

II. The Teachings of Jesus Especially Emphasize That He Wants the Last Person Saved, With None Left Out

We have already shown that many times in the Bible God has expressed His concern for the whole world to be saved. Christ is the "light of the world," the "Saviour of the world," "the Saviour of all men, especially of those that believe." Christ is the "Light, which lighteth every man that cometh into the world." Since He has been lifted up on the cross, He draws all men to Him, we are told. God is "not willing that any should perish, but that all should come to repentance." God "commandeth all men every where to repent." God so loved the whole world that He gave His only begotten Son. He sent not His Son into the world to condemn the world, but that the world through Him might

be saved. The Scriptures give overwhelming proof that God
wants the whole of mankind.

But some of the teachings of Jesus go to great detail
to show that it is the last unconverted person that He is
the most concerned about, the one that men would leave
unsaved.

The three parables in Luke 15 all unite in this great
emphasis. The scribes and Pharisees murmured because the
Lord Jesus received sinners, and seemed even more concerned about the vilest sinner, the worst lost ones. At the
complaint of the Pharisees and scribes, Jesus gave these
three wonderful parables on the lost sheep, the lost coin,
and the lost boy.

Jesus said, "What man of you having an hundred sheep,
if he lose one of them, doth not leave the ninety and nine
in the wilderness, and go after that which is lost, until he
find it?" The good shepherd would not be satisfied to have
only some of the sheep. He wanted all, the last one. He
wanted not only the good sheep, but the bad sheep. It is
the one last lost sheep which Jesus emphasizes here. And
surely He means that as long as one poor sinner is outside
the fold of mercy and salvation the tender heart of God is
grieved and God's Spirit is seeking! God never provided for
any person to be lost!

A woman had ten pieces of silver and lost one. Only
one was lost, and she had nine pieces left. But she lit a
candle and swept the house and searched diligently until
she found the one lost piece of silver. So, according to the
dear Saviour, God wants the last lost person in the world to
be saved.

A certain man had two sons. One was a faithful, obedient boy; the other turned out to be prodigal, a wastrel, a
heartbreaker for his father. But the father wanted the lost
boy fully as much as he wanted the boy who stayed at home.
The Bible does not picture God as having some people selected for salvation and others selected for damnation. The
Bible does not picture God as satisfied with only a few
saved. The emphasis throughout the teachings of the Gos-

pels is that the Lord Jesus wants the last and most un-
likely and most sinful person in the world saved. God never
planned for any person to be lost.

III. The Emphasis Throughout the Scriptures That All Should Choose Right Shows That Everybody Has the Freedom of Will to Decide to Be Saved or Not to Be

There is one thread of thought that runs throughout
the Bible, one persistent teaching which never varies. It
is that man may choose right or wrong, may choose to obey
or to disobey, may choose to believe or disbelieve, may
choose to be saved or to be lost. That teaching begins with
the story of Adam and Eve in the Garden of Eden. Both
could obey God and continue in perfect happiness in the
paradise which God had prepared for them. They ought not
eat of the forbidden fruit, the fruit of the tree of the knowledge of good and evil. But they had the ability to do so.
Though they were warned of disastrous results, yet they
were still left on their own responsibility. They could obey
God, or they could listen to Satan. They could trust the
Lord about the results, or they could, in unbelief and rebellion, disobey and die. First Eve, then Adam, chose to
eat of the forbidden fruit. Both had the free choice.

That teaching goes straight through the Bible, occur-
ring again and again, until in the last chapter in the last
book of the Bible, the Scripture says, ". . . And whosoever
will, let him take the water of life freely" (Rev. 22:17). On
moral questions, mankind is left with solemn warnings and
with tender entreaties, but with the freedom to choose. To
ignore that teaching will lead to heresy as well as to sin.
A man may not choose the color of his eyes; a man cannot
add one cubit to his stature; a man cannot select his own
father or mother, or the place of his birth. There are many,
many things about which men have no choice, things which
are decided in God's loving provision, so that man cannot
change them. But on moral matters, matters of right and
wrong, matters of loving and serving God or of rebellion and
disobedience and willful unbelief, men and women all down
through the ages have been able to take their choice.

Spurgeon, the great English preacher, called himself a Calvinist, but he did not go into the barrenness and fruitlessness of the hyper-Calvinists who hold that some men are predestined, compelled, to reject Christ. Preaching on the inspired prophecy that Hazael would murder the king of Syria and take the throne, Spurgeon said:

"God foreknew the mischief that he would do afterwards, when he came to the throne; and yet that foreknowledge did not in the least degree interfere with his free agency. Nor is this an isolated and exceptional case. The facts most surely believed among us, like the doctrines most clearly revealed to us, point all of them to the same inference. The predestination of God does not destroy the free agency of man, or lighten the responsibility of the sinner. It is true, in the matter of salvation, when God comes to save, His free grace prevails over our free agency, and leads the will in glorious captivity to the obedience of faith. But in sin man is free—free in the widest sense of the term, never being compelled to do any evil deed, but being left to follow the turbulent passions of his own corrupt heart, and carry out the prevailing tendencies of his own depraved nature."—pp. 30, 31, Vol. 13, *Spurgeon's Sermons.*

In Deuteronomy 30 the Lord solemnly warns Israel of the tremendous choice set before every man. In verses 15 to 20 God says:

"See I have set before thee this day life and good, and death and evil; In that I command thee this day to love the Lord thy God, to walk in his ways, and to keep his commandments and his statutes and his judgments, that thou mayest live and multiply: and the Lord thy God shall bless thee in the land whither thou goest to possess it. But if thine heart turn away, so that thou wilt not hear, but shalt be drawn away, and worship other gods, and serve them; I denounce unto you this day, that ye shall surely perish, and that ye shall not prolong your days upon the land, whither thou passest over Jordan to go to possess it. I call heaven and earth to record this day against you, that I have set before you life and death, blessing and cursing:

therefore choose life, that both thou and thy seed may live: That thou mayest love the Lord thy God, and that thou mayest obey his voice, and that thou mayest cleave unto him: for he is thy life, and the length of thy days: that thou mayest dwell in the land which the Lord sware unto thy fathers, to Abraham, to Isaac, and to Jacob, to give them."

Note this remarkable statement: "See, I have set before thee this day life and good, and death and evil." It is obvious here that they are to choose. And they are solemnly warned of punishment and disaster "if thine heart turn away, so that thou wilt not hear . . . ." It is a plain matter of the will, of choice. In that case, He says, "I denounce unto you this day, that ye shall surely perish . . . ."

Then read again that solemn warning in verse 19, "I call heaven and earth to record this day against you, that I have set before you life and death, blessing and cursing: therefore choose life, that both thou and thy seed may live."

By turning to God in penitent love, one may choose life and live. One may reject life and choose death by turning away from God. It is a matter of the will, a matter of the choice. If the Bible is an honest book, and if God is an honest God, men must themselves, of their own choice, decide for or against God. In this matter they are not coerced; they are pleaded with, and they are warned, but they may go right or wrong.

That kind of choice is offered Israel again in the days of Joshua. In Joshua 24:14, 15, hear this solemn warning and ultimatum from God:

"Now therefore fear the Lord, and serve him in sincerity and in truth: and put away the gods which your fathers served on the other side of the flood, and in Egypt; and serve ye the Lord. And if it seem evil unto you to serve the Lord, choose you this day whom ye will serve; whether the gods that were on the other side of the flood, or the gods of the Amorites, in whose land ye dwell: but as for me and my house, we will serve the Lord."

We are clearly told that Joshua himself made the choice.

". . . But as for me and my house, we will serve the Lord."
The others are exhorted also to fear the Lord and serve Him,
and to put away idol gods. But they were plainly told that
they were to "choose you this day whom ye will serve."

They had freedom of choice. God wanted their love and
allegiance. He had Joshua present the matter thus to them.
The blessed Holy Spirit had it written down for succeeding
generations. It is clearly intended in any honest interpretation of this Scripture that people are urged to choose and
may choose between right and wrong, between God and idols,
between obedience and disobedience, between faith and unbelief.

Repeatedly throughout the Bible the appeal of God is to
the will, the choice. For example, Ezekiel 18:31, 32 says,
"Cast away from you all your transgressions, whereby ye
have transgressed; and make you a new heart and a new
spirit: for why will ye die, O house of Israel? For I have no
pleasure in the death of him that dieth, saith the Lord God:
wherefore turn yourselves, and live ye."

". . . Why will ye die . . . ?" God asks. Evidently dying
is a matter of choice, and God plainly says, "I have no pleasure in the death of him that dieth . . . ." Therefore, He
implores, ". . . turn yourselves, and live ye."

Again in Ezekiel 33:11, the Lord says, "Say unto them,
As I live, saith the Lord God, I have no pleasure in the death
of the wicked: but that the wicked turn from his way and
live: turn ye, turn ye from your evil ways; for why will
ye die, O house of Israel?"

God does not want anybody to be lost. No one is predestined to be lost. God has "no pleasure in the death of the
wicked," and again He asks the question, "Why will ye die, O
house of Israel?" In other words, He might properly say,
"Why do you choose to die?" It is left up to your own choice.
You may choose to live or you may choose to die. God does
not want you to die. If you go on and die in sin and away
from God, it is because of your own wicked choice of the will.

In Psalm 81:11-13, the lament of the Lord against His
people is because of this same willful turning to sin and away
from God: "But my people would not hearken to my voice;

and Israel would none of me. So I gave them up unto their own heart's lust: and they walked in their own counsels. Oh that my people had hearkened unto me, and Israel had walked in my ways!"

Do you see that it was the will of people not to listen to the voice of God and not to please Him? As a result, God gave them up to their own sins and the results of sin, but His heart was grieved. "Oh that my people had hearkened unto me...," God said. Is God deliberately deceiving? Had God decided ahead of time that these must go on in sin and could not repent? No, His heart grieved for their sin, and all the more because it was a deliberate, independent choice against God.

So in Proverbs 1:25 God complains of sinful people, "But ye have set at nought all my counsel, and would none of my reproof." It is a matter of the will to disregard God's commands. Men do have a choice and exercise their choice. God may decide some matters for men but never moral matters of right and wrong. Always man can obey or disobey. Man can love God or hate God. Man can trust Christ or reject Him. God grieves when men turn away, but they still have the choice in all moral matters, all matters of right and wrong.

When Jesus spoke so wonderfully to disbelievers and rebels among the Jews of His day, many rejected His sayings and asked for further proof. To those Jews who sought to kill Him, Jesus said, "And ye will not come to me, that ye might have life" (John 5:40).

The complaint is not that they could not come, that they were too dead in sins to know or choose; rather, it was simply that they could choose and did choose, willfully, wrongly, to reject Christ and go on in their sins. THEY WOULD NOT COME!

God in that last invitation in the Bible said, ". . . the Spirit and the bride say, Come. And let him that heareth say, Come. And let him that is athirst come. And whosoever will, let him take the water of life freely" (Rev. 22:17). But He was saying what He had said throughout the Bible. On matters of right and wrong, God leaves man to choose. All could be saved. God invited all to be saved. But God has not made man an automaton. God has not made man a machine. He wants the deliberate and loving choice of the free will. He wants men to love Him because they choose to love Him and because He is worthy of love. He wants men to obey Him from the deliberate choice of the heart. When men will not come to Christ for salvation, God is grieved, but God is not responsible. Throughout the Bible, the teaching of the freedom of will to choose for Christ is taught. And that shows that no one is predestined to be lost.

We would do well to enter into the heart of the Saviour and see how He feels. In Luke 9:56 Jesus said, "For the Son of man is not come to destroy men's lives, but to save them." All the predestination in the Bible is intended to save men, not to damn them. God's plan through the ages is and the coming of Christ on the cross was all to express the heart of God and the heart of His Son. Jesus did not come to destroy, but to save. Those who picture Jesus as wanting people to go to Hell do not understand His spirit any more than James and John when they would have called down fire from Heaven to consume the Samaritans.

Chapter VII

God's Grace Not Irresistible

The Scriptures show that enlightened, convicted men do resist God, do thwart the grace of God. Men who could be saved, who are set apart by the blood of Christ, men who are bought, resist the Holy Spirit. God's grace is offered all, but is not irresistible, as Calvin taught.

One of the five points of this man-made philosophy of extreme Calvinism is the doctrine of "irresistible grace." By this term Calvin meant, and hyper-Calvinists today mean, that God intended for only a limited number of people to be saved, that the atonement of Christ paid for the sins of only this limited few (the doctrine of "limited atonement," as extreme Calvinists call it) ; that those who are predestined to be saved cannot resist the grace of God, cannot reject the Saviour but are certain to be saved. For this reason extreme Calvinists are not generally burdened about soul winning since, they say, the grace of God is "irresistible."

So if we can show that the Bible teaches that men do resist the grace of God, do resist the moving and conviction of the Holy Spirit, we have proved that extreme Calvinism is simply not true, that it is unscriptural, a man-made philosophy contrary to the Bible. But the Bible and human experience alike prove that men do resist the Spirit of God, do thwart divine grace. Therefore some could be saved who are not saved, and the atonement is for all.

In the seventh chapter of Acts we find Deacon Stephen, a Spirit-filled man of God, speaking before the Sanhedrin and Jewish elders. And Spirit-filled Stephen said, "Ye stiffnecked and uncircumcised in heart and ears, ye do always resist the Holy Ghost; as your fathers did, so do ye. Which of the prophets have not your fathers persecuted? and they have slain them which shewed before of the coming of the Just One; of whom ye have been now the betrayers and murderers" (Acts 7:51, 52).

To these Jewish leaders Stephen said, "Ye do always resist the Holy Ghost." So here were people some of whom had seen Jesus and heard Him preach, others who had heard Peter the apostle at Pentecost, others who had heard Stephen and other Spirit-filled men preaching with great power so that "the word of God increased; and the number of the disciples multiplied in Jerusalem greatly; and a great company of the priests were obedient to the faith" (Acts 6:7). And what had these done? They were stiffnecked and uncircumcised in heart and ears, that is, they were stubborn in their rebellion against God. They were deliberately "uncircumcised in heart and ears," remaining unconverted. And this resistance against the Holy Spirit went to such length that as they heard Stephen preach, "they were cut to the heart, and they gnashed on him with their teeth," and then they took him out of the city and stoned him and killed him!

Men *did* resist the Holy Spirit. These particular men had done so year after year under great moving of the Holy Ghost.

And Stephen said, "As your fathers did, so do ye." So Stephen says that all the way from Abraham through the history of the Jewish nation down to the time of Christ and those same Jewish elders, unconverted Jews had resisted the Holy Spirit!

Thus we must believe, taking the Word of God at face value, that God calls people who do not come. God convicts people who will not repent. God's Spirit moves people to be saved, but they will not be saved.

One of these same Jewish leaders who heard Stephen speak was Saul of Tarsus. Oh, how he hated this new sect of Christians! And now with that hate flaming in his heart and the zeal of Judaism he set out to arrest Christians at Damascus. You see, Paul up to this time was resisting the Holy Ghost, so much so that later God said to him, "It is hard for thee to kick against the pricks" (Acts 9:5). So people do kick against the pricks of God's Holy Spirit. People do resist the call of God. People do resist God's grace and do thwart God's offer of mercy. And that means that those who are not saved could have been saved. Those who reject Christ could have accepted Him. God offers mercy to those who will not have it. Those who go to Hell go, not because God wanted them to go, nor because they were predestined to go to Hell, but they go to Hell because they would not heed the moving of the Holy Spirit on their hearts, and they would not repent when God commanded them to repent. They would not follow the light that God gave them.

Again in Hebrews 10:29 we find the clear statement that men resist God, that sometimes men who are convicted and moved to get saved will not be saved.

Read Hebrews 10:28 and 29 together: "He that despised Moses' law died without mercy under two or three witnesses: Of how much sorer punishment, suppose ye, shall he be thought worthy, who hath trodden under foot the Son of God, and hath counted the blood of the covenant, wherewith he was sanctifed, an unholy thing, and hath done despite unto the Spirit of grace?"

First, note that God says the damnation of a lost sinner is illustrated by the stoning of rebels against the Mosaic law in the Old Testament. Those who "sin wilfully after that we have received the knowledge of the truth" (verse 26) are ready for judgment for rejecting the truth. Notice that the sin mentioned is willful sin and this involves a certain freedom of the will to sin or not to sin. (I speak not now of the taint in our carnal nature, but in the actual choice of right and wrong, the choice of receiving Christ or rejecting Him.) So a willful sinner under the Mosaic law, at the mouth of two or three witnesses, was stoned. But then God warns us, "Of how much sorer punishment, suppose ye, shall he be thought worthy, who hath trodden under foot the Son of God, and hath counted the blood of the covenant, wherewith he was sanctified, an unholy thing, and hath done despite unto the Spirit of grace?"

Verse 29, here quoted, teaches so clearly that men who turn down Christ do it deliberately and that the punishment is because of the willfulness of their sin. Notice these sins:

1. They have "trodden under foot the Son of God."

2. Such a man has "counted the blood of the covenant, wherewith he was sanctified, an unholy thing."

This may mean either of two things. It may mean that every lost sinner is in some sense sanctified by the death of Christ, that is, potentially set apart for God. Since Jesus is potentially "the saviour of all men," but "specially of them that believe," as we are expressly told (I Tim. 4:10), then the blood of Jesus, potentially, sets apart every sinner in the world for God. That is saying no more than I Corinthians 15:22: "For as in Adam all die, even so in Christ shall all be made alive." Every poor sinner is bought by the blood of Jesus. He is the propitiation "for the sins of the whole world" (I John 2:2).

Or some will think that "the blood of the covenant, wherewith he was sanctified" refers to the blood of animal sacrifices which Jews gave. They think that every Jew was thus sanctified or set apart by a covenant of blood. But if so, that does not change the essential meaning. If every Jew was set apart by bloody sacrifices, then those bloody sacrifices typified the blood of Christ and the blood of Christ surely went as far as the blood of bulls and goats! This Scripture plainly teaches that the blood of Jesus Christ has set apart every sinner for salvation. Some do not accept the salvation that is offered. Jesus is "the Saviour of the world," although not all the world will take Him as Saviour. Jesus is "the propitiation for our sins: and not for our's only, but also for the sins of the whole world" (I John 2:2), although some people do not accept the blessed gift that is given. So here the Scripture is teaching that the blood of Christ has purchased people for salvation who do not take salvation.

But the third thing this Scripture says about such a sinner who rejects Christ is that he "hath done despite unto the Spirit of grace." The blessed Holy Spirit who calls the sinner and whom he resists is insulted and abused by the Christ-rejecting sinner!

Oh, poor lost sinner, when you go to Hell you must remember that you have trodden under foot the Son of God. You must remember that when you go to Hell you counted the blood of Jesus shed for you an unholy thing. In Hell, poor lost sinner, you must remember that you were called and pleaded with and convicted and enlightened by the Holy Spirit, but you insulted that Spirit, you did "despite unto the Spirit of grace."

We are talking here about the grace of God which is so freely offered to sinners by the Holy Spirit. And sinners resist and reject that grace of God and insult the Holy Spirit who pleads with them, so teaches the Word of God.

So every lost sinner could be saved. The death of Christ met the requirement and paid for his sins. The precious blood is a holy thing which would pay the entire debt. The Holy Spirit of God calls in grace but sinners refuse. This Scripture does not teach "irresistible grace," but it teaches the grace of God offered to all men so that all could be saved and all ought to be saved.

Second Peter, chapter 2, is given up to a discussion of false prophets. The whole 22 verses are on this subject and the chapter starts off with this statement: "But there were false prophets also among the people, even as there shall be false teachers among you, who privily shall bring in damnable heresies, even denying the Lord that bought them and bring upon themselves swift destruction."

These false teachers bring in damnable heresies "denying the Lord that bought them."

Here is the strange statement that even false teachers are bought by the blood of Jesus Christ.

This chapter goes to great detail to show that these false prophets are lost people, certain of the judgment of God. Verse 3 says of them, "Whose judgment now of a long time lingereth not, and their damnation slumbereth not." The rest of the chapter tells us how God who spared not the angels that sinned, but cast them down to Hell, will not spare these false teachers. Verse 5 tells us that as God destroyed the ungodly in the flood, so He will destroy these false teachers. Verses 6-8 tell us as God destroyed Sodom and Gomorrah, so He will destroy these false teachers. These false teachers are described in verse 12 "as natural brute beasts, made to be taken and destroyed." Verse 17 speaks of these false teachers as "wells without water, clouds that are carried with a tempest; to whom the mist of darkness is reserved for ever." These false teachers are ungodly men who will go to Hell. They are men "even denying the Lord who bought them."

Nothing could more clearly show that these men are included in the atoning death of Christ, they are included in the grace of God which would save everyone. But they resist the grace of God, they reject the call of the Spirit, they exercise the freedom of their wills to reject Christ and be lost.

Men do resist the will of God and go to Hell, who could be saved. And that shows the folly of this man-made philosophy of hyper-Calvinism. It shows the falsity of this human doctrine of "limited atonement," this human doctrine of "irresistible grace," this doctrine that some are "foreordained to reprobation" as others are "foreordained to be saved."

I do not need to call attention to the fact that those of us who are saved in most cases long resisted the call of God. In Genesis 6:3 we are told that the Holy Spirit strives with men and then sometimes ceases striving. In Acts 24:25 we are told how as Paul "reasoned of righteousness, temperance, and judgment to come, Felix trembled . . . ." No doubt this blessed Spirit of God convicted Felix and spoke to his heart. He waited for a convenient season and, we suppose, kept on waiting and went to Hell. But he cannot say that he might not have been saved. He can never say that the Spirit of God did not call him, did not convict him, did not show him his need.

The very fact that Christians are warned against the sin of quenching the Spirit (I Thess. 5:19) and are solemnly warned, "Grieve not the holy Spirit of God" (Eph. 4:30), shows that the grace of God is not irresistible. Man has certain moral freedom of choice. Lost men must choose whether or not they will be saved. And saved people must choose whether or not they will more perfectly follow the Lord than they do.

God's grace offers salvation to all men. All could accept it; some do not.

Chapter VIII

Bible Doctrines Show Hyper-Calvinism Morally Impossible

There are inherent spiritual reasons why God could not predestinate one to do right and another to do wrong, one to be saved and one to be lost.

Those hobby-riders who believe that God predestined some people to be saved and that they will be saved by God's coercive grace, and that others are predestined to be lost and cannot be saved because of God's deliberate choice, are foolishly wrong, desperately wrong. They are wrong in having a doctrine that cuts clear across so many emphatic Scripture statements inviting all to be saved, showing that Christ died for all, that God is not willing that any should perish. But they are also wrong in that they go against great fundamental, logical scriptural reasons inherent in the nature of God and of man, inherent in the nature of right and wrong. It is a moral impossibility for God to coerce man to do wrong and choose for man ahead of time that he must repent or that he cannot repent.

I do not mean simply that human logic proves hyper-Calvinism morally impossible. I mean there are great doctrinal truths, inherent and basic truths, clearly taught in the Bible which make hyper-Calvinism morally impossible.

I. The Bible Pictures Man as a Free Moral Agent Capable of Choice, Morally Responsible

First, there is the nature of man as it is pictured in the Bible and as it actually exists. God breathed into Adam's nostrils and he "became a living soul." He was made in the image of God. And what is this about man that is God-like? He is a reasoning creature with a moral responsibility, a conscience toward right and wrong, with the freedom of choice in right and wrong. Man is superior to beasts in mental powers, but the simple truth is that now men can make an electric computing machine which can go through complicated mental processes of adding, subtracting, remembering, judging, hundreds of times faster than man can do it! But the electronic brain, the Univac, has no will, no conscience, no consciousness of right or wrong. Hence it has no personality. It lacks the God-given moral nature of man.

Why did God allow Adam and Eve to fall, and so bring a curse on the whole human race? It was inherent in the kind of being that God created; man must be allowed to choose. But knowing that some man sometimes would choose wrongly, God planned with His Son before the world began to offer an atonement for the salvation of sinning men! So Christ is "the Lamb slain from the foundation of the world"

(Rev. 13:8). But the ability to fall was in the very nature of man.

God made a man who could love or who could hate. He made a man who could do right or do wrong. He made a man who could turn to God, and serve, and follow and trust Him, or who could hatefully, wickedly reject Christ and God. It is inherent in the very nature of man.

This is apparent all about us. Strangely enough, despite all the influence that we may put about him, every child has a certain willfulness which is an essential part of his ego, his personality. He will or he won't! That will may be trained for God. If we begin in time, by God's loving mercy, the child may be won to trust Jesus Christ and be saved, and get a new heart, or sin may harden his heart. But we can never change the fact that every child which comes into this world has the ability to choose on moral matters, though he may be influenced, and does choose in moral matters.

But if people have that choice and exercise that choice in other matters, it is certain that they also exercise it in the matter of accepting or rejecting Christ.

Sometimes people who are mentally unsettled, sometimes violent, arrogant, ruthless, make life intolerable for themselves and others. In such cases, doctors have sometimes performed a brain operation called lobotomy, by which one lobe of the brain is severed from the rest of the brain. Strangely, part of the will is gone. The patient may become docile, easygoing, without the drive and push he had before. One part of the man's independent moral nature has been tampered with. Though it is only partial, even so, it is sometimes disastrous. Intelligent physicians everywhere debate on the matter and feel that lobotomy is a last resort for a man mentally unbalanced because of a certain overburdening sense of responsibility or sense of self-will. But the simple fact is that when one tampers with a man's independent will, he has tampered with a man's personality, his very being and soul. Independent choice of the will in moral matters, right and wrong, is an essential part of the nature of mankind. Since man's God-given nature is such as it is, it would be morally impossible for God to force man's decision on moral matters arbitrarily, causing one man to do right and causing another man to do wrong, without giving the man freedom of choice.

What makes a thing right, and what makes it wrong? The rabid evolutionists, who make no real distinction between man and beast, and who reject divine creation of man in the image of God, tend toward the doctrine that there is no absolute right or wrong. If we are all the product of evolution, who could blame man for some beastly instincts? Is the wolf that kills a sheep a murderer? Are cows and horses, mating indiscriminately, guilty of adultery? Is the crow that gets in the corn field a thief? Is the rabbit that nibbles the lettuce in the garden a thief? You see, if you leave out the moral nature of man, you have ruined the Bible concept of right and wrong.

But right and wrong are facts based on the nature of God and the command of God.

But how could it be wrong for a man to reject Christ, if he had no power to accept Him? How could God bring a lost sinner to judgment for his sins and his Christ-rejection if the man had no choice? Don't you see that the very nature of right and wrong, as taught in the Bible and proceeding from God Almighty, makes it so that God cannot coerce the human soul on these matters?

But here is, I think, the strongest possible argument that God could not have predestined some to be lost and some to be saved. If God had predestined some to be saved, there would be no virtue in their love. Their righteousness would be only an outward formal righteousness with no heart virtue in it. But if God predestined some to sin, to reject Christ, to refuse repentance, to hate the Bible and God, then God Himself would be the creator of sin, would be partaker of man's sin and wickedness, and partner in that wickedness, God forbid! It is an unthinkable and wretched doctrine!

Does the Scripture not say that "God cannot be tempted with evil, neither tempteth he any man" (Jas. 1:13)? The God who is "no respecter of persons" puts in every human being a moral nature which must choose and does choose right or wrong. And eventually every such person who comes to the age of accountability must choose to accept or reject Christ, to seek God or run from God. Thus it would be morally and spiritually impossible for God to predestinate some to be saved and predestinate others to be lost, except as He acts on His foreknowledge of who will turn to Christ. The nature of man, the nature of right and wrong, the nature of God Himself, forbid it.

II. Calvin's Supposition of "The Absolute Sovereignty of God to Save or Damn Without Any Human Choice" Is Scripturally Untenable

Calvin and those who follow Calvin love to use the term, "the absolute sovereignty of God." And by this they mean, as they have said in print again and again, that God had decided before the world began who would be saved and who would be lost, that He made the choice without any reference to man's choice or will, that man has nothing to do with it. They say that God has chosen some for Hell and they cannot be saved, cannot seek God, cannot repent. They say that God has chosen others to be saved and that with them God's grace is irresistible. The point is that the only decisions made are made by God, that God was and is absolutely unlimited and, therefore, that God takes all the moral responsibility in this universe.

First, let us remind you that Calvinists use many terms which are unscriptural and antiscriptural. They speak of "irresistible grace," though the Bible never uses that term. They speak of "limited atonement," though the Bible never mentions such a doctrine nor uses such a term. They speak of "total inability" of a man to repent or seek, though the Bible says nothing like that.

Why can we not use Bible terms to mean Bible doctrine? Why not let *grace* mean that sweet nature of God to love and seek and forgive sinners who do not deserve it, instead of saying "irresistible grace" and making it mean the whim of a despot which is coercive fiat instead of compassionate invitation?

The Bible says many wonderful things about God, but it never says that God is an absolute unlimited sovereign. That is man's idea, not a Bible teaching.

Do you think God is unlimited? Then do you not remember that the Scripture says, "God, that cannot lie . . ." (Titus 1:2). There are some things that God, being good and holy, cannot do. He cannot lie. He cannot do wrong.

The simple truth is that God is righteous and righteousness excludes unrighteousness. Some qualities of God necessarily limit other characteristics of God. God made man in His own image. That meant that God assumed certain obligations. A good and holy God cannot now act as if He had no moral responsibility and no interest in the race He has created.

God throughout the Bible makes certain grave and glorious promises. But God, like all honest men, is bound by His promises. When a man signs a note at the bank, then he is honor bound to pay the money he has promised on a certain date. When a man enters a contract with the electric company or the gas company or with the city for water supplies, then he enters an obligation which necessarily binds him. No good man can do as he pleases about paying debts, except he can please to do right and pay them. And as a good man cannot rightfully repudiate an honest contract of promise or obligation or debt, so a holy and righteous God cannot now ignore promises He has made.

When God takes a sinner to His heart, saves him, changes him, forgives him, and puts His own nature in the new convert, then God has limited Himself. When I married and brought children into the world, I assumed obligations that an honest man cannot evade. I made holy vows at the marriage altar. That meant that I renounced the right to certain freedom which an unmarried man has. I obligated myself about the support of a family, the rearing of my children. To suppose that God Himself, a righteous, holy God who has made covenants and promises, who has created a universe and a race for which He is responsible—to say that such a God is therefore unlimited in moral matters of right and wrong, is foolish.

God is love and love limits absolute sovereignty. Jesus Christ is the truth, and the truth itself sets up barriers beyond which even God, who cannot lie, must not and cannot go.

A God who wrote the Bible cannot now act as if He did not write it. God who made man and put him on this earth cannot now act as if He never made man. God who made covenants with Adam and Noah and Abraham and David and the nation Israel cannot Himself ignore those covenants. The God who filled the Bible with the sweet entreaties for sinners to be saved cannot now act as if He had no responsibilities for those invitations and promises to sinners.

No, the way hyper-Calvinists use terminology about the "absolute sovereignty of God" as if God Himself were not bound by any moral obligations, as if He were not bound by His own nature, as if He were not bound by His acts and promises, is a false emphasis, contrary to that clearly taught throughout the Bible.

III. Calvin's Doctrine That All Decisions Are Made By God Ahead of Time Is a Fatalism Irreconcilable With the Scriptures

We know, of course, that God determines many things ahead of time. The Bible clearly teaches that again and again. But on moral matters, matters of right and wrong, men are allowed to decide for themselves. God does not coerce the moral nature of some to do right and coerce the moral nature of others to do wrong.

Hyper-Calvinists by "natural sovereignty of God" mean that God Himself makes all the decisions that are made, and that men do what they are compelled to do, right or wrong. According to such Calvinists, the sin and fall of Adam and Eve were planned ahead of time by God (Calvin's Institutes 11:207, 208). But if a lost sinner cannot make any moral decision except as he is compelled by the Spirit of God to, then a Christian cannot pray unless God has fore-ordained him to pray. By that doctrine a Christian cannot do any good deeds except as he is compelled to do them.

But that would mean that when God rewards a Christian, there is no honor and no righteousness in it. People would then be rewarded for what they did not choose of themselves to do. But if this strange man-made philosophy of hyper-Calvinists were true, then the judgment seat of Christ would be a mockery.

And if hyper-Calvinists were right, then it would be foolish to pray. God would have already determined who will pray and who will not. And God would have already determined the answer. And man would have no choice of his own in the matter, either for good or for bad.

There is no essential difference between the unbelieving fatalism of Calvinists and the fatalism of Moslems or other heathen people. Essentially Calvinism would teach that there is no real right or wrong, no moral responsibility for men and women. Essentially Calvinism would teach that the laws of sowing and reaping, of rewards and punishments, are not valid, honest laws. All the fundamental doctrines involved in sowing and reaping, in praying and getting the answer, in winning souls or leaving them to go to Hell because of our cold, compassionless hearts—I say these basic fundamentals are denied by Calvinism. Yes, Calvinism is a moral impossibility in the light of Bible doctrine.

IV. The God of the Bible Has Compassion and Personal Love for Individuals

God is love. He so loved the world that He gave His Son. And this love is not impersonal and academic, but it is individual. Jesus said that the shepherd who lost one sheep out of one hundred loved that one with a holy devotion and suffered to bring it back to the fold. And so Jesus teaches that He loves every poor sinning individual. So the Bible teaches that Jesus wept over Jerusalem and that even now He "is not willing that any should perish, but that all should come to repentance."

We know of course that God's love is for us as free individuals. God's love cannot do wrong. God cannot take to Heaven unrepentant sinners; to do so would be to violate His own holiness and righteousness. God's love is so great that He gave His Son to die in the torments of the cross, but love does not mean that God can rightly take a Christ-rejecter to Heaven. It does not mean that unrepentant sinners ought not to be sent to Hell and must be sent to Heaven. When we say that God is love, we do not mean that God is not bound by righteousness and holy responsibilities. God loves men, and God grieves when men go to Hell. So the Bible clearly teaches.

But hyper-Calvinists say that God planned it all so! They say that God planned the fall of Adam and Eve. They say that before the world began, God damned some people to torment and made it so they could never repent, could never be saved. So they tell us that all who sinned were intended to sin, that they could not help sinning. If the grace that saves some sinners is "irresistible grace," then according to hyper-Calvinism the damnation of those who do not repent is "irresistible damnation." That is, they say that God is responsible and gladly planned for some people to go to Hell.

But the God of the Bible is not so pictured. He is a God of compassion, of mercy. He must let unrepentant sinners go to their natural doom, when sinners themselves take the responsibility and will not come for mercy and forgiveness. God's righteousness demands that. But God's righteousness, according to the Bible, does not demand that God compel people to sin and then damn them for sinning, that He make it impossible for them to repent and then burn them in Hell because they could not repent.

Jesus wept over Jerusalem. Does not that mean that He wanted them to be saved? Yes, He plainly said, "How often would I have gathered thy children together, even as a hen gathereth her chickens under her wings, and ye would not!" (Matt. 23:37). Then here are people lost whom Christ did not want lost! Here are people who are damned and condemned, but it was by their own choice and not by the choice of the Lord Jesus.

The Lord Jesus said about Judas Iscariot, "It had been good for that man if he had not been born" (Matt. 26:24). So that means when a man goes to Hell, he goes forever; far better that Judas Iscariot had never been born than to have rejected the Saviour and betrayed Him. But hyper-Calvinists would tell us that God planned it so, that Judas had no choice. If that be so, then God Himself would be responsible for millions of people in eternal torment, when it would have been better for them never to have been born! That makes God responsible for wrong. And that is wholly hateful to the sense of the Scriptures.

V. The Fact of the Unpardonable Sin Proves That Many Are Convicted and Invited Who Are Never Saved

The very fact that the Bible speaks of an unpardonable sin proves that hyper-Calvinism is wrong and unscriptural, as I think I can show you.

In Matthew 12:31, 32 Jesus said the following about the unpardonable sin:

"Wherefore I say unto you All manner of sin and blasphemy shall be forgiven unto men: but the blasphemy against the Holy Ghost shall not be forgiven unto men. And whosoever speaketh a word against the Son of man, it shall be forgiven him: but whosoever speaketh against the Holy Ghost, it shall not be forgiven him, neither in this world, neither in the world to come."

I think that the unpardonable sin is a somewhat deliberate and final rebellion against the wooing of the Holy Spirit who would turn a lost sinner to Jesus Christ. But whatever the unpardonable sin is, it is still unpardonable. In the above Scripture Jesus makes it clear that up until a man "speaketh against the Holy Ghost" he might be forgiven. After that sin, his sins are unpardonable.

That means that people go to Hell who are not foreordained to go to Hell, but could have been forgiven, does it not? In Revelation 14:9-11 we are told plainly that every person who takes the mark of the antichrist will go to Hell. We are told, "If any man worship the beast and his image, and receive his mark in his forehead, or in his hand, The same shall drink of the wine of the wrath of God, which is poured out without mixture into the cup of his indignation;

and he shall be tormented with fire and brimstone in the presence of the holy angels, and in the presence of the Lamb." Now if the Bible means what it says, those who will worship the antichrist and receive his mark thus pass beyond the pale of forgiveness. They doom themselves certainly for Hell.

But if the worship of the Beast dooms a man as unpardonable, he could have been pardoned before. But if that be true, then some who could have been saved go to Hell. They go not because they were predestined to go to Hell, but because they committed a certain final sin that shut them off from mercy, from the call of God, from the moving of the Spirit, a sin that made it impossible that they should ever repent and be saved. But if that be true, they did not go to Hell because they were predestined to go to Hell, but because of their sin.

In Genesis 6:3 before the flood God gave a warning. "And the Lord said, My spirit shall not always strive with man . . . ." He indicated that after many, many warnings the Holy Spirit would retire from those who lived before the flood and let them all go hardened and impenitent to their doom in the flood! We are told in I Peter 3:18-20 that Christ by the Holy Spirit in the days of Noah preached to those who are now in prison. So we learn that some heard the preaching of Christ by the Holy Spirit and were not saved. We were not told that Noah did the preaching, but Christ through Noah. We are not told that the people heard Noah, but they heard the Spirit of God. God spoke to their hearts. But God's Spirit quit calling and left them to their doom.

Does not that mean that one can be convicted, can be enlightened, can be moved toward God and yet resist and go to Hell? If so, then men go to Hell not because they were predestined to go to Hell, but because they deliberately choose to resist the Spirit and reject Christ. And this again shows that all men are somewhat enlightened and dealt with by God's Spirit, though many are never saved.

We are told that Felix trembled when Paul preached to him (Acts 24:25). Doubtless he was deeply convicted. But he waited for a more convenient season. So millions of other sinners have been convicted by the Spirit and perhaps have trembled, but still did not repent, and went to Hell. But that means they went to Hell because they *would not* repent, not because they could not. People do not go to Hell because they are predestined to be damned. They go to Hell because they do not repent and will not let Jesus Christ save them.

Many, many great principles in the Scriptures make it certain that God must leave men free choice to accept or reject, to be saved or to be lost. Men cannot blame God for their sin nor for their damnation when they insist on remaining in sin.

Chapter IX

God Predestinates Those Who Will Trust in Christ to Land Safe at Last in Heaven!

Hyper-Calvinists have a bad teaching, a false doctrine. And it comes from a misapplication and a misunderstanding of a very few Scriptures, and a total ignoring of many others. No Scripture ever said that God predestinates anybody to be lost. Not a verse of Scripture in the Bible says that some are predestined to be saved whether they choose to trust in Christ or not. No, such a teaching is only inferred by a misapplication of certain Scriptures. But God does teach that He has determined ahead of time to take all who will trust Christ safe to Heaven.

There are some Scriptures which refer to God's selection of individuals for a certain destiny, and His rejection of individuals or nations for that destiny. Such Scriptures are taken to mean that God selects some to be saved and some to be lost.

For example, in Romans 9:11-13 the Scripture plainly

says that God chose Jacob to be the head of the nation Israel, and rejected Esau for that purpose.

*"(For the children being not yet born, neither having
done any good or evil, that the purpose of God according to
election might stand, not of works, but of him that calleth;)
It was said unto her, The elder shall serve the younger. As
it is written, Jacob have I loved, but Esau have I hated."*

All the context, the Scripture quoted from the Old
Testament, and the historical passages in Genesis dealing
with the matter, plainly show that this is the meaning. God
chose Jacob to be the head of the nation who would inherit
the promises given to Abraham and his seed; He rejected
Esau for this purpose. That had nothing to do with whether
either or both of the men would be saved. Neither was predestined to be saved, and neither was predestined to be
lost.

It is true that in Exodus we are told that "the Lord
hardened Pharaoh's heart." But from the context and the
discussion in Romans 9:14-24, it is clear that Pharaoh was
already a wicked rebel against God, a murderer, the en-
slaver of God's people, rejecting every call, every demand
that God made. So God raised him up for destruction. He
hardened Pharaoh's heart in his refusal to let the children of
Israel go. But He did not harden Pharaoh's heart toward
the matter of salvation and God. That was already done before God brought him to destruction. Pharaoh had hardened
his own heart.

Then in a few places in the Bible God's people are
spoken of as being elected or ordained. But always it is with
the meaning that God has plainly promised and ordained
that those who trust in Christ shall be saved and that He
will keep them and bring them safe to Glory.

The most prominent and most explicit of these passages
is Romans 8:28-34, and we should read it very carefully.
What a glorious Scripture it is! This Scripture means what
it says and says what it means.

*"And we know that all things work together for good
to them that love God, to them who are the called according*

to his purpose. For whom he did foreknow, he also did predestinate to be conformed to the image of his Son, that he might be the firstborn among many brethren. Moreover whom he did predestinate, them he also called: and whom he called, them he also justified: and whom he justified, them he also glorified. What shall we then say to these things? If God be for us, who can be against us? He that spared not his own Son, but delivered him up for us all, how shall he not with him also freely give us all things? Who shall lay anything to the charge of God's elect? It is God that justifieth. Who is he that condemneth? It is Christ that died, yea rather, that is risen again, who is even at the right hand of God, who also maketh intercession for us."

We believe this Scripture encompasses all the truth that is revealed to us about predestination, election, and foreordination as it relates to salvation. There are other Scriptures which briefly mention the subject, but the above Scripture in Romans 8 is fuller and more explicit.

I. The Only Foreordination the Bible Speaks of Regarding Salvation Is for Good, Not Bad, for Salvation and Not for Damnation

Everything in the passage under discussion, Romans 8:28-34 and its context, is addressed to Christians, not to lost people. It brings assurance, not despair. It is "to them that love God" (vs. 28). The only predestination discussed here is predestination "to be conformed to the image of his Son" (vs. 29). The only predestination and foreordination spoken of here is for those who will be saved, not for those who will be lost.

God's children are often called "the elect." Leaving out some passages that probably refer to Israel as a select, chosen nation, we find still many Scriptures which very clearly refer to Christians as God's elect. See Luke 18:7, Romans 8:33, Colossians 3:12, I Timothy 5:21, II Timothy 2:10, Titus 1:1, I Peter 1:2, I Peter 2:6, II John 1, and II John 13.

In I Peter 5:13 certain Christians are called "elected."

In I Thessalonians 1:4 and II Peter 1:10 the "election" of Christians is mentioned.

Now, if God has elected more people to be damned than those chosen to be saved, and if He has determined their damnation, their "reprobation," as hyper-Calvinists say— isn't it strange that it is never mentioned? All the election as far as the doctrine of salvation goes in the Bible is about Christians, never about the lost!

The Bible often speaks of people elected for Heaven: It never speaks of anybody who is elected or chosen to go to Hell. Reader, do you not think it wise for us to keep the emphasis just where the Bible keeps it? Then we must not teach that God has chosen anybody to be damned. The Bible does not teach that.

The term "ordained" is used frequently in the New Testament. Only one time, I believe, is it used in reference to salvation. Acts 13:48 speaks of "As many as were ordained to eternal life." Note that here the reference is to people being saved, not people being damned. Of course God knew who would be saved, who would trust Christ, and these were saved. But it is certainly impressive that not once in the Bible are we ever told that anybody is ordained or elected or selected or foreordained to be damned, predestined to go to Hell.

In Romans 8:29, 30, quoted above, twice the term "predestinate" is used about Christians. Again in Ephesians 1:5, 11 Christians are spoken of as being "predestinated." But again there is no such word used anywhere about people being damned, foreordained or predestined to be lost with no chance to be saved. Such a doctrine is not taught in the Bible. The election for eternity is of Christians.

It may be that proud and haughty people with carnal pride and selfishness may then infer that they are so much more loved of God than others that they are chosen and others are rejected, and they may infer that as God has chosen them for Glory, He has chosen others to be lost. But that inference is not even hinted at in the Scripture. It comes from a serious misunderstanding of the Scriptures and perhaps from a heart either calloused toward all the promises and offers of mercy of God, or ignorant of them. No one has a right to teach from these Scriptures that God has predestinated some people to be lost so that they cannot repent and cannot be saved. That simply is not taught in any Scripture in the Bible!

Charles Spurgeon, in his sermon on Isaiah 55:1, "Ho, every one that thirsteth, come ye to the waters," says:

> "Now it does not say, 'Every one, except—except —except—' No, no. Here is an amnesty published without exception or exemption."

Again that prince of preachers says:

> "Well now, I believe the doctrine of election. I thank God I do. It is a precious doctrine, and let me tell you, dear friend, that the doctrine of election shuts nobody out, though it shuts a great many in. 'But I may not come and trust Christ.' How do you know? God says you may, and He tells you you shall; in fact, He says, 'He that believeth not is condemned already, because he hath not believed,' thus making it a sin not to believe; so you really have such a right to believe that it becomes even your duty. Whatever the doctrine of election may be, or may be meant to be, we will not talk of that just at present, for it is quite certain that it cannot contradict any plain practical direction of Scripture. Here is a plain text, which no one can gainsay, 'Whosoever believeth in him is not condemned.' If, then, you believe on Jesus Christ, you are not condemned, election or no election. But let me tell you, if you believe in Christ you are one of His elect, and it is because He elected you that you come to believe in Him; it is because He chose you that you are led to desire Him and made to accept Him. Let not that doctrine ever terrify you, or provoke your distrust, for if you rightly understand the revelation, it is rather a finger beckoning to Christ than a specter that should intimidate you, or drive you away from Him."
> —pp. 153, 154, Vol. 13, *Spurgeon's Sermons.*

I would that all who try to quote Spurgeon as an extreme Calvinist would follow Spurgeon in saying that predestination, as taught in the Bible, is always for good, never for bad. No one was ever made so he must reject Christ. God is not willing that any should perish. The Bible doctrine of election is, as Spurgeon understood it is, "rather a finger beckoning to Christ than a specter that should intimidate you, or drive you away from Him."

No, the predestination taught in the Bible, particularly in Romans 8:28-30, is for those who will be saved and these Scriptures are written for the comfort and assurance that God will take them safely on to Heaven and will finish the work that He has begun.

II. The Only Foreordination and Predestination to Salvation Is Based Simply on God's Foreknowledge of Who Will Trust Christ for Salvation

There is a divine order in this Scripture which we dare not overlook. Read verses 29 and 30 again, in the wonderful eighth chapter of Romans, and see where predestination starts:

"For whom he did foreknow, he also did predestinate to be conformed to the image of his Son, that he might be the first-born among many brethren. Moreover whom he did predestinate, them he also called: and whom he called, them he also justified: and whom he justified, them he also glorified."

The only people that God predestinates to be saved are those whom He did foreknow, that is, those who, in His infinite knowledge, God knows will, when given the opportunity, come to trust in Christ to be saved. It is not that predestination *causes* people to trust Christ and be saved. No, they are only predestinated to be saved because God knows that they will put their trust in Christ. Predestination is based wholly on God's foreknowledge.

In Romans 8 Paul says about God that "whom he did foreknow, he also did predestinate . . ." (Rom. 8:29). The same truth is taught by the Apostle Peter in I Peter 1:2. There he addresses those who are the "elect according to the foreknowledge of God the Father . . . ."

You see, here it is twice expressly stated that the election of Christians is based on the foreknowledge of God; that is, their election is not the cause of their being saved, but they are predestinated simply because God knows they will trust Him when they hear the Gospel. Remember this clear Bible teaching twice plainly stated in the New Testament, that predestination is based on God's foreknowledge. God predestinates people to be saved whom He knows will turn to Him in repentance and faith.

To suppose that God, on some whim, predestinates one to be saved by "irresistible grace" so that those saved can have nothing to do with it until it is accomplished, and that others are predestinated to be damned, irresistibly so they cannot change it—that idea is not taught in the Scriptures. No, in the Bible, predestination for eternity is for Christians only, and predestination is always for salvation and never against salvation, and it is based on the foreknowledge of God.

To our ignorant, finite minds, limited by our meager knowledge and experience, it is impossible to understand fully the foreknowledge of God. My knowledge is measured in terms of time. Once I was a child. I grew, I had experiences, I learned. When I was a child I did not know what I know as a man. When I was a single man I did not know what I know as a husband and father, with many years of experience in the problems and responsibilities that go with a family. People, events, circumstances come into my knowledge and become a part of me. So, until I can become infinite in mind like God, I cannot fully understand God's foreknowledge of all things.

But with God there is no past or future, but an eternal present. Before the world began, He knew every person who would be born and what they would do. The future He knows perfectly; the past He remembers perfectly. The past is as clear to God as the present. But the future is also as clear as the present. So before the world began, God gave His Son, and in the mind and plan of God, Christ was a Lamb slain before the foundation of the world (Rev. 13:8). Did God know when every sinner would trust in Him? Yes,

He knew that before the world began, and He knows it now. And the only predestination regarding salvation is that God has determined that those who trust in Him will be carried on straight through to Heaven! Briefly that is the sum and substance of predestination, foreordination, and election as far as they relate to salvation at all.

Mark it carefully. The Bible does not hint that God arranges it so that anyone will be saved without making the deliberate choice to turn to Christ and trust Him in penitent faith. God foreknows the moral choices of men, but God does not predestinate those choices! God made man in His own image, a moral being. It is a part of the nature of man that he has a conscience, that he is accountable in matters of right and wrong, that he must choose in right and wrong. A holy God could not arrange for a man to always choose the right without taking away the man's personality, his will, his God-like soul. And God could not arrange for a man to do wrong without being a partaker of man's guilt and becoming a sinning God! When God created man and created laws of right and wrong, and gave commandments and instructions and invitations to man, He then cannot coerce the will of man as if man were a robot, a machine to be manipulated.

God can bring the pressure of loving invitation or stern warnings, to cause a man to weigh the consequences and the moral issues and decide. But God cannot make all the moral decisions in the universe without leaving Himself to be the only moral being in the universe. When He creates other moral beings, accountable, subject to laws and subject to rewards and punishments, then God Himself thus deliberately limits His control over those beings. Without understanding this, one cannot understand the problem of evil in this world. Evil is in the universe because God, a moral being, created other moral beings who must be accountable. These beings have sinned and brought evil and sin into the world. If God did not leave man's will uncoerced to choose right or wrong, then God Himself would be responsible for the sin and evil in the world.

So God knows ahead of time who will trust Him, but

God does not compel them to trust Him. God knows who will reject the Saviour, but God does not cause them to reject the Saviour. God's foreknowledge does not involve the control of the will and does not do away with individual responsibility for moral actions and decisions on the part of mankind.

Here we are told that "whom he did foreknow, he also did predestinate to be conformed to the image of his Son." God knows who will trust the Saviour in penitent faith and be saved, so He plans ahead of time that these will be called by the Holy Spirit when they hear the Gospel, that they will be justified or transformed, then that one day they will be glorified at Christ's coming, with resurrected bodies and their salvation made perfect and complete. Then, praise the Lord, every person who ever put his trust in Jesus Christ as Saviour will appear in the image of God's only begotten Son, and Jesus will be really, literally, "the first-born among many brethren." And all of these brethren (and sisters), perfect, glorified, worthy children of God, will be fit for the companionship and delightful presence of God forever!

III. God Makes Sure to Call Everyone Who Will Hear, Everyone Whom He Knows Will Accept the Blessed Invitation to Be Saved!

See here the wonderful grace of God. "For whom he did foreknow, he also did predestinate to be conformed to the image of his Son, that he might be the first-born among many brethren. Moreover whom he did predestinate, them he also called . . . ."

It does God dishonor and is a perversion of truth to make this Scripture contradict all the great promises and invitations of God. God loved the whole world. God would "have all men . . . come unto the knowledge of the truth." He is "not willing that any should perish, but that all should come to repentance" (II Pet. 3:9). "God . . . commandeth all men every where to repent" (Acts 17:30). Christ, lifted up, draws all men to Him. The Holy Spirit convicts the whole world. ". . . And whosoever will, let him take the water of life freely" (Rev. 22:17). No Scripture is of any private interpretation, but every verse in the Bible fits into one general plan. So this verse simply carries further the blessed truth that God's seeking, loving heart does all that a loving, just, and holy God can do to get all men saved.

God knows who will trust Him, so He sees to it that every such person in the universe is called!

Cornelius, the Roman centurion of the Italian band, a man from Rome who spoke Latin, earnestly sought God. He had no Bible, had heard no preacher. Yet in Acts, chapter 10, we are told that God sent an angel from Heaven to tell Cornelius where he could find a preacher who would tell him and his household how to be saved! How eager God is to see that every person who will hear the Gospel is called and the way of salvation is made clear.

In the interior of Africa the chief of a tribe had a dream. According to his dream, a great canoe with white wings arrived at a seaport many miles away. On the great canoe was a man with a strange white face who told people of the true God. The African chieftain was so impressed that he sent some of his men to the seacoast. And there truly came a great ship and a missionary from America. They found an interpreter and told the strange story. The missionary came to the African village. The chieftain was not saved, but many in his village were. Why? Because God knew that there were hearts there open to the Gospel, and His loving heart would move heaven and earth to give them a chance to hear the Gospel and be saved! Everyone whom God foreknows, He calls.

We have already seen that in some sense Christ, lifted up, draws all men in the world to Him (John 12:32). We have seen that He is the "Light, which lighteth every man that cometh into the world" (John 1:9). But God goes further than that. He makes sure that everyone who follows what light he has can have more light. Everyone whose heart is open to truth hears the truth. Oh, God goes to such length to save everyone who would be saved that it is wicked to blame Him if any man remains lost!

Chapter X

The Harm Done by Hyper-Calvinism Heresy

A doctrine cannot be unscriptural without doing actual harm. God's way is right; man's way is wrong. And when the doctrine on the matter of salvation is wrong, it is certain to hinder the cause of Christ. So the human philosophy of hyper-Calvinism, the doctrine of hyper-Calvinism, the doctrine that every detailed event that happens in all the world was foreordained of God and had to happen, every sin was ordained of God, every act of a Christian or of a sinner, and that everyone was either foreordained to be saved before he was born, without having any free choice in the matter, or was damned without any possibility of his being saved—that doctrine is hurtful and has done great harm to the cause of Christ.

I. Hyper-Calvinists Actually Hinder and Oppose Gospel Preaching and Soul Winning

If it seems shocking to accuse any group of opposing Gospel preaching and hindering soul winning, a little thought here will show that hyper-Calvinists must inevitably oppose soul-winning activities of those who try to get every sinner to repent, of those who offer salvation freely as purchased on Calvary for every person. Hyper-Calvinists disagree violently with the thought that lost sinners can repent and that it is a man's own fault if he will not turn to Christ and be saved.

For example, the book, *Whosoever Will*, by Professor Herman Hoeksema, is written to answer the evangelical and literal interpretation of Revelation 22:17—". . . And whosoever will, let him take the water of life freely." Professor Hoeksema says that "whosoever will" may come, but that a sinner cannot even *will* to come unless he is fore-ordained to come to Christ. And he takes up invitation after invitation to sinners given in the Bible, to explain that they do not mean what they appear to mean, but that "That work is absolutely divine. Man has no part in it, and cannot possibly cooperate with God in his own salvation. In no sense of the word and at no stage of the work, does salvation depend upon the will or work of man or wait for the determination of his will."

And what is the attitude of Professor Hoeksema toward gospel preaching and evangelism? He says, on page 91:

"But thanks be to God, the Light of the world does not shine by the grace and good will of the darkness; it is sovereign. It is not dependent on the will of the sinner: it is irresistible. It is not contingent upon the begging and pleading and contortions of a modern hawker of Jesus, but sends its piercing and illuminating rays whithersoever it wills." Professor Hoeksema speaks slightingly of "the begging and pleading and contortions of a modern hawker of Jesus."

Again, on pages 108 and 109, Professor Hoeksema says:

"All the more peremptory it is to inquire into the meaning of coming to Jesus because of the abominable travesty of it that is presented by many a modern self-styled evangelist and revivalist. And it is high time that the Church, that is the custodian of the gospel, and to whom alone is given the commission to preach the Word, should raise her voice aloud in protest against the widely practiced evil of hawking Jesus, and of presenting Him as the cheapest article on the religious market, that may either be procured or rejected by the sinner at will. To come to Jesus is, according to a very usual phrase, to accept Him as our personal Saviour."

In the same paragraph, Professor Hoeksema continues:

"O, indeed, they admit that salvation is of grace, and some of these hawkers of salvation even prattle of sovereign grace; but this grace is, nevertheless, presented as enervated and paralyzed if the sinner refuses its saving operation!"

And then follows a rather caricatured account of evangelistic preaching and of the public invitation to accept Christ, which the hyper-Calvinist despises. Professor Hoeksema continues as follows:

"And this gives rise to all the evils of which Arminianism gone wild affords daily demonstrations from pulpits and over the air. The sinner's power to accept or reject Jesus receives all the emphasis, and the result is that the act itself of coming to Christ is presented as something natural and very simple. All that is required of the sinner is to raise his hand, or to come to the front, or to kneel down by the radio, and repeat after the preacher: 'I accept Jesus as my personal Saviour,' and the matter is settled."

Notice the sectarian bias, the misrepresentation in this passage. In the first place, some soul winners are Arminian and some are not. Most of the Presbyterians are not Arminians. Practically none of the Baptists are Arminians. Most of those in the independent, fundamental movement, aligned with the Bible institutes, the independent Christian colleges and magazines, are not Arminian. To say that to invite sinners to come to Christ is Arminianism is a bald misrepresentation. It is a part of the fallacy of this man-made philosophy that there are only two plans of salvation held by Christians, Arminianism and hyper-Calvinism.

Again, what a sorry and evil misrepresentation of evangelistic preaching is this word by this hyper-Calvinist! The Professor says, "All that is required of the sinner is to raise his hand, or to come to the front, or to kneel down by the radio, and repeat after the preacher: 'I accept Jesus as my personal Saviour,' and the matter is settled." Any man who ever publishes a book or professes to speak with any authority in religious matters ought to know that no reputable soul winner in the world teaches that one is saved by raising his hand or saved by coming down to the front, or saved by kneeling down by the radio, or saved by repeating the phrase, "I accept Jesus as my personal Saviour." That it is such a bald-faced misrepresentation and so often repeated by hyper-Calvinists shows that there is a deadly enmity toward real soul winners, and that this bias, this prejudice, this enmity leads them to misrepresent the facts.

Every great evangelist in the world accepted either by Arminians or by others who believe in the eternal security of a believer knows there must be a heart repentance, a turning away from sin in the heart, and a personal trust, faith, committal to Jesus Christ. I have read the sermons of the greatest soul winners of the past. I have known the great soul winners from Billy Sunday and Gipsy Smith on down to the present. I know, and every informed man knows that none of them ever thought one was saved by raising a hand, by coming to the front, by kneeling down by the radio, or by repeating any phrase in the world. I do not believe that Professor Hoeksema thinks so. If he does think so, it shows how blinded he is by his animosity toward gospel preaching. But that kind of thing is taught theological students, is preached in the pulpits, is open opposition to gospel preaching everywhere that hyper-Calvinists have a good hearing.

Dr. H. A. Ironside in his book, *A Short History of the Brethren Movement,* tells how John Nelson Darby, the principal founder and authority of the whole Plymouth Brethren movement, was invited by D. L. Moody to preach in the Chicago Avenue Church of which Moody was pastor, now called Moody Memorial Church. But in the midst of the week, Darby became so incensed at Moody's insistence on saying that "whosoever will" should come and be saved, that Darby broke off the services, did not finish his announced series, and left. Darby was himself a hyper-Calvinist, as some of his followers are. He did not like the preaching of Moody. He refused to let his influence be known as favorable to Moody, at that time a young evangelist. Hyper-Calvinists hinder the preaching of the Gospel and oppose it by evangelicals.

The late Dr. Lewis Sperry Chafer, founder and long president of Dallas Theological Seminary, was a devoted follower of Darby, and, like Darby, a hyper-Calvinist. And what was his attitude toward evangelism and principal soul winners? One who wishes may read his book, *True Evangelism,* which plainly says that the evangelist himself is a false force in evangelism, that any request for a sinner to hold his hand for prayer, or to come forward in public confession of Christ, or to take any other action in connection with his faith, is a false force in evangelism. And Dr. Chafer said that evangelists give the public invitation as a simple way to get more obvious and visible results to get more money. I had a long correspondence with Dr. Chafer on this matter, and he said plainly in private letters that he had in mind the methods used by R. A. Torrey and J. Wilbur Chapman, as well as others. And in churches led by Dr. Chafer's pupils, there has been a tendency not only to shut out evangelists, but to avoid the public invitation and to sneer at so-called emotionalism, and otherwise hinder evangelists and evangelism.

I have preached all over the South and again and again in communities where the Primitive Baptists, hyper-Calvinists, had a foothold, and there was open opposition to the preaching of the grace of God, open opposition to urging sinners to repent, open opposition to the revival campaigns, to the public invitation for people to receive Christ and confess Him. Again and again I have seen parents interfere with their own deeply convicted young people who wanted to be saved, because the parents were hyper-Calvinists and were so desperately opposed to soul-winning efforts and to the ardent proclamation of the Gospel.

I have found the same situation to exist wherever Dutch Reformed people have had widespread preaching of their predestination doctrine. In several areas in Michigan one who comes to have revival campaigns will meet the stolid indifference of a population which has been taught that they need not fret, because if they are to be saved they will be saved without being active in the matter at all, and if they will be damned, they cannot help it. The soul winner will there have also the active opposition of those who oppose the straight-out preaching of the invitations of Christ for sinners to repent, to trust Him, to come to Him. Hyper-Calvinism opposes the warmhearted, Spirit-filled effort to win souls.

I will never forget how shocked I was in Texas to meet the family of a Primitive Baptist preacher. This man would preach two hours on predestination, but I found that his grown sons were unconverted, and the father was not only totally indifferent about that matter, but insisted that no one else should try to win them to Christ. That is the attitude of hyper-Calvinism toward gospel preaching and the gospel invitation.

II. Hyper-Calvinism Is Either Indifferent to or Opposed to Foreign Missions

Of course there will be exceptions. Some people who are hyper-Calvinists do love Christ in their hearts and so feel His moving of concern for sinners. And most hyper-Calvinists will profess that they believe in the preaching of the Gospel to all the world. But in actual practice, hyper-Calvinism cuts the nerve of soul winning on the foreign mission field as it does at home.

Did a great foreign mission program arise through the teaching and preaching of John Calvin? Many hyper-Calvinists will regret this fact, and some will deny it, no doubt. But the simple truth is that today those most active and most burdened about soul winning on the foreign field among Presbyterians are not those who believe in Calvin's doctrine of predestination. In fact, nine out of ten Presbyterians do not believe it, and the great mission program of Presbyterians was not built by hyper-Calvinists.

As the Wesleyan revival spread in England, of course it affected many others besides Methodists and many besides Arminians. Missions are not primarily an Arminian enterprise. Most of the Bible-believing, soul-winning Christians in the world are not Arminian, except among Methodists and among some Lutheran groups. But few soul winners are unreserved Calvinists. Hyper-Calvinism does not produce a passion for soul winning.

Do you remember when William Carey pleaded with the hyper-Calvinists in Presbyterian Scotland to send missionaries to India? And do you remember that the chairman rose and said, "Sit down, Mr. Carey. If God wants to save the heathen He will do it without your help!" That is the attitude of hyper-Calvinists toward missionaries and foreign missions, when "missions" means soul winning.

In the summer of 1956 I was in Japan, addressing some 500 missionaries of the Evangelical Missionaries Association of Japan. Dr. Donald Barnhouse came along, and was given some afternoon meetings at times when services had not been planned. And this hyper-Calvinist Presbyterian, Dr. Barnhouse, said to the missionaries in my presence, "If people are not saved at your mission station, do not blame yourself. Do not fret. That is not your fault. What a torment I should have if I thought the saving of souls depended upon my faithfulness! No, if God is going to save them, He will save them, and if they are lost, it is not your fault." Those are not the exact words, but that is the exact sentiment of his message.

Again he told the missionaries, "If you are saved now, there never was any danger of your being lost, because God had determined to save you."

Would you say that that kind of talk inspires missionary passion and burden for souls? It does not!

Consciously or unconsciously, actively or passively, hyper-Calvinism opposes and hinders foreign missions as it hinders soul winning at home.

III. Hyper-Calvinism Is a Spirit-Deadening Philosophy That Ruins Many Individual Christians

This man-made philosophy of hyper-Calvinism appeals to a certain kind of mind. It appeals to the brilliant student more than to the ordinary person. It appeals to the arrogant and proud more than to the humble. It has had deadly affect on many who have taken up this fad, this philosophy.

I know a man who did a flaming work as an evangelist. He trained in evangelical schools. Then he held revival campaigns in a day when we evangelists had to fight our way, had to endure all kinds of abuse and suspicion and slights. I have often felt that his preaching was among the most moving and penetrating I had ever heard. The man had graduated *summa cum laude* from his college and in seminary was a tremendously brilliant student.

But I saw, bit by bit, a certain arrogance coming into his ministy and into his personal life. Perhaps the fact that in secret he held on to the tobacco habit had something to do with it. I do not know. Perhaps the influence of one strong, arrogant and worldly individual who made great impressions on him had something to do with it. I do not know. But little by little he began to lose out in evangelism and then began to teach and preach hyper-Calvinism more and more. Now he would sometimes preach and give no invitation for sinners to accept Christ. Now he would sometimes say, "I do not know whether God intends for any of you sinners here to be saved or not." Soon he was utterly ruined. The waste, the sidetracking, the personal ruin which came to that man's ministry and Christian life are heartbreaking. It was brought by hyper-Calvinism and the stirring up of an arrogant spirit and the loss of concern for sinners that go with hyper-Calvinism.

I am thinking of another young man. The president of the university from which he graduated told me that he was perhaps the most brilliant student they had ever graduated. But here, too, this brilliant mind met a philosophy which appealed to him. It appealed to him all the more because he felt that many could not understand it. It was too deep for most people, but not for him. He went into hyper-Calvinism. And then he went into all kinds of excesses—speaking in tongues, attacks on other Christians, etc. Hyper-Calvinism meant ruin in his case, disaster in personal life, disaster to his ministry.

Some Christians, like Charles H. Spurgeon, have nominally held to Calvin's position without spending much time on it and without having their lives ruined by it. Spurgeon lived in a time when the two great clashing systems of religious thought were Arminianism and Calvinism. Spurgeon believed in the great doctrines of grace, of man's fallen condition, that man could be saved only by grace without works, and that God keeps those He saves. So Spurgeon nominally accepted Calvinism. And so there is an occasional reference to election and predestination in Spurgeon's preaching. But it was with him not a major matter. He had a burning heart, the fullness of the Spirit, and so he pressed always to get sinners saved. Unfortunately, those who followed Spurgeon in his Calvinism did not follow him in the soul winning. Those who followed him in the soul winning, thank God, did not follow him in the Calvinism. But Spurgeon was never an active and strong Calvinist in the sense of Calvin and the Westminster Confession of Faith, though he nominally accepted the system of Calvinism. Whitefield was a Calvinist in the sense that he believed in salvation by grace and the security of the believer, but I find little evidence that he believed and preached predestination of sinners to Hell as Calvin himself did.

Hyper-Calvinism and evangelism are opposites. Wherever there has been a great breaking out of revival, whether the Finney revivals or the D. L. Moody revivals, or the Billy Sunday revivals, there has been a retreat of the people from hyper-Calvinism. Wherever common people have been led to study the Bible, not as an exposition of the Westminster creed, not to find certain doctrines of their sect or denomination, but impartially, undenominationally, as the open Word of God, in interdenominational or undenominational surroundings, then hyper-Calvinism has lost ground. Warmhearted soul winning prospers when hyper-Calvinism diminishes, and the opposite is sadly true.

How sad, then, to see young men from fundamental Christian colleges attend a seminary where their minds will be twisted by this human philosophy, where their concern for souls will ebb away and where they will come to worship mind and logic, instead of loving and following the simple Word of God.

It is true that Darby and Arthur Pink, his disciple, and some others of the Brethren have been hyper-Calvinists. But that is not characteristic of the Bible institute movement of the Bible conference movement in America, nor of the modern missionary movement, nor of mass evangelism.

Hyper-Calvinism is the enemy of soul winning, of missions, it tends to satisfy the heart not willing to pay the price for soul winning. It appeals to the arrogant, the proud, and tends toward spiritual ruin for individuals.

For a complete list of books available from the Sword of the Lord, write to Sword of the Lord Publishers, P. O. Box 1099, Murfreesboro, Tennessee 37133.